PRAISE FOR *WHAT ADDICTS KNOW*

"In this revealing and readable book, Christopher Lawford sets out 10 lessons of recovery—drawn from his own struggles and those of others—that can help everyone enhance and enrich their lives."

—JOSEPH A. CALIFANO, JR.,
founder of CASAColumbia, The National Center on
Addiction and Substance Abuse at Columbia University

"In a way, we're all addicts—addicted to the fears and limitations of the world in which we live. By shedding light on the realities of recovery, Lawford sheds light on how anyone can best achieve the mindset of wisdom and inner peace."

—MARIANNE WILLIAMSON,
New York Times bestselling author of *The Age of Miracles*
and founder of The Peace Alliance

"Not to be overlooked in the wisdom contained within is the acknowledgment of the enormous personal courage to bare all for all to benefit. To have had secrets and give them up into public view as markers on Life's Highway, and to face degrading thoughts by thoughtless people, is far greater illustration of moral character than it sounds. Chris is Witness; he is authentic in his pain, insights, and desire to help."

—RICHARD DREYFUSS, actor

"The insights in *What Addicts Know* are unparalleled. Christopher Kennedy Lawford provides a unique perspective on the enlightening lessons gleaned from recovering addicts' experiences. This is a book that will change the way we think about the wisdom of healing."

—ED BEGLEY JR., actor

"With his 10 lessons, Christopher Kennedy Lawford eloquently explores how the insights offered by recovering addicts can benefit individuals in any walk of life."

—CHRIS MATTHEWS, host of MSNBC's
Hardball and author of *Tip & the Gipper:*
When Politics Worked

"Simply reading and seriously considering the list of 10 lessons at the beginning of this extraordinary book will move your life toward wholeness."

—RICHARD CHAMBERLAIN, actor

"Knowing is not enough; we must apply. Willing is not enough; we must do. Mr. Lawford's book offers such knowledge and we can all benefit from it."

—JOHN LARROQUETTE, actor

"As we learn from Christopher Kennedy Lawford, 'What Addicts Know' is a lot. We would never wish addiction on someone we love, but Lawford shows us that those in recovery from addiction have gone through the eye of a needle. It happens to those of us whose loved one is addicted, too. When the addicted come out the other side, they appreciate life in a new way. They never take for granted those they love. They are empowered to reach goals they never thought they could attain. They can lead full lives free from the pain that plagued them and the disease that controlled them. Addicts' families change, too. In *What Addicts Know*, not only does Christopher Kennedy Lawford help us to heal, but to thrive. As he has consistently, Lawford blazes new trails, guiding and inspiring us."

—DAVID SHEFF, *New York Times* bestselling author of
Beautiful Boy: A Father's Journey Through His Son's Addiction

"Like his previous books, in *What Addicts Know*, Chris Lawford provides an essential and important perspective. In this book, Lawford reminds us that, too often, observers dismiss people with addiction struggles whole cloth—as if they have little to offer. However, despite or perhaps because it is a demanding master, addiction shapes people's existing skills and teaches new ones. In *What Addicts Know*, Lawford describes a repository of vital life skills and lessons—derived from the experience of addiction—that are essential for living a full, satisfying, successful, and happy life. Lawford puts the resilience, compassion, acceptance, problem solving, independence, empathy, hope, creativity, risk-taking, forgiveness, and the many other essential gifts of people who have struggled with addiction on display for all to see. Lawford describes a path to enlightened recovery that is essential for everyone: finding an authentic sense of self and learning to connect it to purpose within the world-at-large. Ultimately, *What Addicts Know* is a book for everyone interested in finding a place for themselves, learning more about the human condition, and ultimately advancing their own sense of humanity."

—HOWARD J. SHAFFER, PHD, CAS,
associate professor, Harvard Medical School and director,
Division on Addiction, The Cambridge Health Alliance

WHAT
ADDICTS
KNOW

10 LESSONS FROM RECOVERY TO BENEFIT EVERYONE

CHRISTOPHER KENNEDY LAWFORD

Foreword by Drew Pinsky, MD, Host of HLN's
Dr. Drew on Call

BENBELLA BOOKS | DALLAS, TEXAS

BenBella Books, Inc.
10300 N. Central Expressway
Suite #530
Dallas, TX 75231
www.benbellabooks.com
Send feedback to feedback@benbellabooks.com

Printed in the United States of America
10 9 8 7 6 5 4 3 2 1

Library of Congress Cataloging-in-Publication Data

Lawford, Christopher Kennedy, 1955-
  What addicts know : 10 lessons from recovery to benefit everyone / by Christopher Kennedy Lawford ; foreword by Drew Pinsky.
    pages cm
  Includes bibliographical references and index.
  ISBN 978-1-939529-06-0 (trade cloth : alk. paper)—ISBN 978-1-939529-07-7 (electronic) 1. Addicts—Rehabilitation. 2. Recovering addicts. 3. Substance abuse—Treatment. I. Title.
   HV4998.L394 2014
   362.29—dc23

                                                                    2013027441

Editing by Brian Nicol
Copy Editing by Francesca Drago
Proofreading by Jenny Bridges and
   James Fraleigh
Cover design by Bradford Foltz

Jacket design by Sarah Dombrowsky
Text design by Neuwirth & Associates, Inc.
Text composition by Integra Software
   Services Pvt. Ltd.
Printed by Bang Printing

Distributed by Perseus Distribution
www.perseusdistribution.com

To place orders through Perseus Distribution:
Tel: (800) 343-4499
Fax: (800) 351-5073
E-mail: orderentry@perseusbooks.com

Significant discounts for bulk sales are available. Please contact Glenn Yeffeth at glenn@benbellabooks.com or (214) 750-3628.

This book is dedicated to the millions of men and women, both old and young, who live their lives as inspiring examples of the power of recovery.

CONTENTS

FOREWORD

People are often curious about why I choose to work with addicts. They seem genuinely surprised by my answer. Instead of saying what they might expect (albeit true) that "I do it out of compassion for these suffering souls," I usually express a point of view that catches them off guard.

The truth is, I work with addicts because they are some of the most powerful, richest, most human people you could ever meet. And I don't mean that addicts are necessarily powerful in business or government or rich in terms of material wealth. Most are not. They are rich where it counts most—in character, talent, and life experiences. And perhaps they even excel in relation to something that is more difficult to characterize. Let's just call it *spirit*.

Addicts may do bad things while addicted and feel awful about it afterward. They can test anyone's patience to the max. But once they are solidly in recovery from their addictions, they become incredible survivors and truly wise, because what has happened to them is rather profound.

Though I can give you countless examples of these almost miraculous transformations, let's focus on just one. When I first met Bob Forrest in the late 1980s, he was an international rock star and a horrific heroin addict. He was hardcore. He measured his life by album releases and the deaths of friends, mostly from substance abuse.

Bob was so out of control, so manic and abusive, that some people would actually hide when he showed up. He appeared with me on a radio show in 1988 and was being his usual crazy, abusive self when we got a call-in from a woman who had a very serious question. I don't remember the question or her problem, but I recall that Bob suddenly became very focused and gave her some really reasonable advice over the radio airwaves.

"Bob, you've got something special in you," I told him while we were still on the air. "You might make a great therapist one day if you'd just stop being such a freaking drug addict."

As the years went by, our paths crossed occasionally and I was shocked by his appearance. He was so gaunt it looked like he had AIDS or tuberculosis, and I thought to myself, *Oh, man, this guy is going to die soon.* There seemed to be no way he would survive his addiction.

Fast-forward ten years. I'm giving a lecture for a musician's assistance program somewhere in L.A. and I see this familiar-looking guy sitting in the front row. He asks me several provocative, good questions and I keep trying to place him in my mind: Is that Bob Forrest? The man I had given up for dead?

Throughout that presentation I just kept thinking, *This couldn't possibly be Bob Forrest because he is most certainly dead.* I felt like I was looking at a ghost.

It turned out that Bob had become this amazing, talented, and flourishing recovery guy. He had been in twenty-four different rehab facilities and finally found sobriety in 1996, when most people in his life had given up on him ever surviving.

As you can probably guess, I recruited Bob to work at the psychiatric hospital where I was the medical director. He had a magnificent talent for reaching addicts, and I had the pleasure of watching him develop into a consummate professional. It was actually his frustration with how addicts and their treatments were being portrayed in the press that motivated us to agree to participate in a new reality program that came to be known as *Celebrity Rehab*. If you've seen it, Bob is the cool, smart guy often wearing glasses and a smile, with a fedora parked atop his mop of red hair.

This is the kind of remarkable thing I see all of the time: Someone who seems to be a goner reappears, having come back—way back—from the brink of insanity and death to create a highly productive and contented life for themselves. These are not just random success stories. Those who are in long-term recovery are like missionaries returned from an archetypal journey of suffering and loss, self-discovery and redemption.

I still learn something new every day about the disease of addiction. For example, a friend of mine who was eight years sober admitted to me one time that, despite his life having blossomed in recovery, "I haven't found anything I love as much as drugs and alcohol." That got me thinking about the insidious power of this disease and how, to give up something you love more than anything, you must be deeply motivated beyond belief. How many so-called normal people could face this sort of dilemma and summon the inspiration to wrestle for the rest of their lives with such a powerful demon until it goes into hiding and stays there?

Now you have a glimpse at why addicts intrigue me so much and why I have spent so much time trying to understand the biology of addiction. Addicts are remarkable human beings, and we all have a lot to learn from them.

Take a look at many great poets, artists, and even some of our most famous leaders. Often they are drug and alcohol addicts. Many fighter pilots, extreme athletes, race car drivers, and others who test the limits of endurance are addicts. They are at their best in extremely intense situations.

Why is that? What makes them better survivors? How can many of them continue to function despite parts of their brains being usurped by this disease of addiction? What life skills must they master and from what emotional well must they draw to finally break free? These are some of the questions you will find answers to in these pages.

When Christopher Kennedy Lawford first told me he was researching and writing a book about the "gifts" of addiction and what lessons society can learn from addicts, I knew this was something I would want to read.

In *What Addicts Know*, Chris takes a fascinating look at a completely overlooked subject. It is an important, life-changing book, one that deserves to be widely read and long remembered.

—DR. DREW PINSKY

INTRODUCTION:
THE "GIFTS" OF ADDICTION

A huge percentage of the recovering drug addicts I know seem to have a
few things in common, other than their disease: intelligence, creativity,
individualism, humor, and, yes, they all seem to have or have once had
enormous amounts of ambition.

—KRISTEN JOHNSTON
in *Guts: The Endless Follies and Tiny Triumphs
of a Giant Disaster*

I've dealt with a wide variety of individuals afflicted with the
disease of addiction, and in my estimation they are the most
interesting, fascinating, and gifted people I've come across.
They are also the most challenging; addicts are deviously manipulative and self-absorbed. Their illness causes suffering and pain for
themselves, their loved ones, and the rest of society. Yet from their
struggle comes an opportunity for all.

Recovery is about exposing and healing the darker sides of being
human. And honing the skills necessary for sustained recovery
from addiction reveals a life-enhancing recipe that can benefit
everyone. From the darkness come exquisite, profound gifts.

People who get punched in the face by the eight-hundred-pound gorilla of addiction for decades and who live to tell about it are remarkable human beings on many levels. They are not just survivors, they are teachers. And it's time we all paid closer attention to what they have to teach us about human well-being.

"What does the word 'recovery' mean? What do you get back when you recover? It is yourself," Dr. Gabor Maté told me. Maté is the Canadian physician who authored *In the Realm of Hungry Ghosts: Close Encounters with Addiction.* "There is always a loss of self before addiction starts, either from trauma or childhood emotional loss," said Maté.

We lose that sense of self in childhood. A child cannot soothe her own pain and an infant cannot soothe his own distress. That movement outside of our self for answers is a very natural human movement. We always think something from the outside is the answer. So we use more substances, try to acquire more things, try to achieve more and more. A lot of people who aren't considered to be addicts have the pattern of addicts. Who in our society isn't cut off from themselves? Who doesn't use behaviors to give temporary relief from stress and then can't give up those behaviors? Addiction, or the capacity to become addicted, is very close to the core of the human experience. An addict's recovery of self is a model for everybody in our culture.

That is what this book is ultimately about. Whether or not you are or have ever been an addict, whether or not you know addicts—in fact, even if you consider yourself hopelessly normal and not prone to any kind of addiction or seriously bad habits—you are still at risk and will benefit from the advice in these pages. Before you snicker with skepticism or indignation, let me tell you why I think this is true.

As a culture we've become addicted not only to gambling, drugs, alcohol, and the other usual suspects, but also to technology, the acquisition of material possessions, and every conceivable promise of instant gratification. *More is better* has become society's mantra. We eat more, spend more, take more risks, and abuse more substances . . . only to feel more depressed, unsatisfied, discontent, and unhappy. You may know these symptoms firsthand, or recognize them in the lives of the people you care about.

What we are usually left with is the throbbing emptiness that sets in when the fixation on more brings us nothing but more of the same old feelings of want. Consequently, most of us will do or try just about anything to escape the recurrent stress, frustration, discomfort, and boredom. Those are the warning signs on the road leading to the cliff of addiction and social dysfunction.

We've entered an unprecedented period in human history, a period where technology dominates our waking thoughts and actions, and even our dreams. Smart phones, tablets, and computers; social media and the Internet—all have given rise to an entire new category of dependency and addiction. "There's just something about the medium that's addictive," said Stanford University School of Medicine psychiatrist Elias Aboujaoude in a 2012 *Newsweek* interview. "I've seen plenty of patients who have no history of addictive behavior—or substance abuse of any kind—become addicted via the Internet and these other technologies."

Brain scans support the observation that if you are a technology addict, you feel functionally unable to quit. You may not want to believe it, but the brains of technology addicts resemble those of drug and alcohol addicts—their prefrontal cortexes have been fundamentally altered, and abnormal changes are evident in brain areas that govern decision-making, attention, and self-control.[1]

---

1 Tony Dokoupil. "Is the Web Driving Us Mad?" *Newsweek*. July 9, 2012.

IS ADDICTION THE NEW NORMAL?

Once you realize that the brains of technology and other addicts are different from those of non-addicts, you can't rationally continue believing addicts engage in self-destructive behaviors simply because they are weak-willed or morally flawed. Despite the "Just Say No" antidrug sentiments voiced by former First Lady Nancy Reagan in the 1980s, it's not that simple for addicts. They can't just say no, at least not without help. It's clear that as a species we are rewiring our brains, making ourselves vulnerable to addictive behaviors at an ever-faster pace and in an ever-widening range of ways. The repercussions extend to everyone on the planet.

Though we don't have a fix yet on the number of people who meet the criteria for technology addiction, we get a hint of how extensive the problem could be by looking at how many of us already actively wrestle with other toxic compulsions that negatively affect our health and lives. As I pointed out in my previous book *Recover to Live*, the following well-documented statistics for the United States are stark and revealing:

- 17 million alcoholics
- 19.9 million drug abusers
- 4 million with eating disorders
- 10 million problem gamblers
- 12 million with sexual compulsions
- 43 million cigarette smokers

To complete the picture, we must add in those who also admit to being in recovery from an addiction. At least 10 percent of US adults aged eighteen and older are recovering from drug and alcohol abuse, according to the results of an October 2012 survey by The Partnership at Drugfree.org. Add in those folks recovering from sexual compulsions, gambling addiction, smoking, and food-related issues, and we're probably talking about one in five of all adults, maybe even one in four.

Has addiction become the new normal? I don't know, but we do seem to have become a world of addicts. The toxic compulsions affecting so many people in the United States can be found spreading like a metastatic cancer to practically every culture on earth. To repeat, it's not a crisis of moral weakness and lax discipline. It's a brain disease. Medical science has now conclusively proven that.

Having this disease doesn't necessarily mean the end of your quality of life. As the history of drug and alcohol treatment and recovery demonstrates, people can and do recover—and do so magnificently—emerging from the ordeal far stronger and better prepared for life's many and varied challenges. The ways they do this offer a recovery plan for humanity itself, a plan outlined in the ten lessons in these pages.

TAKE ME TO YOUR ADDICT

While conducting interviews for *Recover to Live*, several treatment experts emphasized how our culture still tries to overlook addicts' contributions to society and the common good. Stigmatized and marginalized, people in recovery from toxic compulsions are too often defined by their problems and not by their accomplishments, such as mastery of the life skills necessary to remain in recovery—a feat made even more remarkable because it occurs within that *more is better* cultural conditioning and overreliance on brain-altering technologies.

What can any one of us, regardless of culture or upbringing, learn from people in recovery from addiction? This book reveals the often inspiring and amazing gifts that addicts must summon and master to maintain the recovery life. But these gifts are usually overlooked by society because of the stigma still attached to the addiction itself.

If you are a non-addict, or "normie," you may be asking, *Where does addiction lead except to jail, a rehab center or hospital, the gutter, or an early grave, right?* Not so fast. Consider what it takes to be a successful addict. You've got to function halfway decently to keep feeding your addiction. You need to summon the inner resources to survive one of the most punishing and treatment-resistant brain diseases known to man, and you must manage to survive long enough to get into recovery and become a productive citizen again.

Addiction is a full-time job that requires a lot of overtime. You're an addict all day, every day, evenings, weekends, and holidays. If your addiction is to illegal drugs, your job is even harder because you need to stay out of jail so you can continue to feed your addiction. To constantly hunt down the drugs and get the money necessary to purchase the drugs, and to do this without losing your freedom, takes a lot of focus and skill. Believe it or not, these skills can become genuine assets when applied to pursuing a healthy lifestyle.

Even if your addiction is to something legal, such as alcohol or the human need for food or sex, feeding that compulsion requires the skill to prevent the rest of the world from knowing about the world you inhabit. So you hide and cover up, make constant excuses, and manipulate other people. To be a successful addict *you have to work at it like your life depends on it.* And often it does.

People recovering from toxic compulsions confront and surmount enormous traumas and challenges in their lives, much like cancer survivors or disaster survivors. And they have more than just their war stories to give us. They've mastered coping and wellness skills we all can strive to develop for healthier and happier lives of our own.

Moreover, many personality traits of addicts are the very qualities we admire and need in our leaders. This isn't just a random theory or an addict's wishful thinking, nor is it based on simply reviewing the long list of addicts throughout history who have had extraordinary lives and monumental achievements. In fact, a growing body of neuroscience research into the dopamine-using circuitry of the brain supports the contention that there is something special about the addict's mental makeup.

"What we seek in leaders is often the same kind of personality type that is found in addicts, whether they are dependent on gambling, alcohol, sex, or drugs," observed Dr. David J. Linden, a professor of neuroscience at Johns Hopkins University School of Medicine, writing in 2011 for the *New York Times*. "How can this be? We typically see addicts as weak-willed losers, while chief executives and entrepreneurs are the people with discipline and fortitude. To understand this apparent contradiction we need to look under the hood of the brain . . . the risk-taking, novelty-seeking, and obsessive personality traits often found in addicts can be harnessed to make them very effective in the workplace. For many leaders, it's not the case that they succeed in spite of their addiction; rather, the same brain wiring and chemistry that make them addicts also confer on them behavioral traits that serve them well."

This idea of beneficial traits lurking in what otherwise looks like unbridled misery is gaining a research foothold in other fields of mental disorders. An October 2012 study in the *Journal of Psychiatric Research* found that creativity is "closely entwined with mental illness."[2]

It's never been a secret in the creative professions that, as a group, they are more likely to suffer from the full range of psychiatric disorders, including addiction, compared to people in other less creative professions. Creatives have felt or seen the

---

2 Simon Kyaga et al., "Mental illness, suicide and creativity: 40-year prospective total population study." *J. Psychiatr Res.* (E-pub) Oct. 9, 2012.

flameouts firsthand. But what is new is a growing professional psychiatric acceptance that these disorders "should be viewed in a new light and that certain traits might be beneficial or desirable," noted Dr. Simon Kyaga, in an interview with the BBC. He and five Swedish colleagues at the Department of Medical Epidemiology and Biostatistics at the Karolinska Institute of Stockholm surveyed more than 1.1 million people, evaluating their psychiatric diagnoses and occupational data over a forty-year period, and found definite evidence of that link between creativity and mental disorders. "If one takes the view that certain phenomena associated with the patient's illness are beneficial, it opens the way for a new approach to treatment," said Dr. Kyaga. This would be a big step forward from the traditional black-and-white view of these diseases, meaning we can therefore "endeavor to treat the patient by removing everything regarded as morbid."

While we shouldn't romanticize people with mental disorders any more than we should people burdened with toxic compulsions, it's now possible to see the potential benefits of these afflictions without, of course, discounting the obvious liabilities and negative repercussions.

How can we separate the toxic side effects of these disorders and compulsions from the "silver linings"—the artistry, talents, and accomplishments? These are all questions worth asking because the answers, as I hope to show in this book, may ultimately benefit society and humanity as a whole.

WHAT WE ALL HAVE TO GAIN

Who among us hasn't yielded to a temptation or craving that we later regretted? Is there any "normal" person who hasn't experienced a temporary loss of control or recurrent obsessive thoughts, even if it's just a musical jingle you can't get out of your head? How can we release more creativity in ourselves without becoming too much of a risk-taker? What are the most important lessons to be learned from the collective recovery experience, and what role can those in recovery play in moving human consciousness forward?

At surface level the problem facing addicts is usually easy to identify: They can't stop engaging in self-destructive behaviors. For self-described non-addicts who also want to improve their lives, the underlying problem or challenge usually isn't so obvious. Yet in digging deeper, we find important parallels to what the addict faces. It can be the feeling of "stuckness," a refusal to change, denial, dishonesty with self and others, a fear of the unknown, unrealistic expectations, feelings of entitlement, and selfishness. It can be a "quick-fix" tendency to self-medicate with toxic substances or to engage in risky behaviors to relieve boredom or stress. Such feelings and tendencies are, if nothing else, human.

Whether in the throes of a full-blown addiction or not, many of us regularly fail to make a connection between our current behaviors and the future consequences of those behaviors, a classic trait in addiction. As individuals no less than as a culture or even a species, we discount the future at our peril. We live beyond our means. We don't save for tomorrow. We postpone getting into recovery from toxic compulsions. We think that Mother Earth will somehow, someday, clean up the environmental messes we make, just like some among us think that time alone will heal all of the emotional messes they've stirred up in their families and their lives.

"We 'normies' have a lot to learn from the lessons demonstrated every day by the recovery community," explained Brenda Schell, program director at the Missouri Recovery Network, a group that works tirelessly to support people in recovery and educate the public about addiction and recovery issues. She continued:

> People in recovery from addictions have overcome things that, before I took this job, I never imagined people could overcome. I've worked with people who were dirt poor, homeless, or came out of a prison or a ditch, and then someone, usually someone in recovery, believed in them and they got the help they needed to build a productive life. I am constantly wowed by that. I just don't see that special bond and connectedness within broader society that I see every day among those in the recovery community.
>
> Those in recovery cultivate an attitude of gratitude. We can all benefit from having an attitude of grace about what we have been given. Addicts in recovery have a willingness to pay it forward. They support each other in the recovery community. Society would certainly benefit from that model of behavior. The Twelve Steps of Alcoholics Anonymous doesn't just pertain to alcoholics . . . How we [feel] powerless over a lot of what happens in our lives. How to take an inventory of ourselves. How to admit the exact nature of our wrongs. Being honest with ourselves and others. Being of service to others. Being a messenger of hope . . . pertains to all of us. These are messages and lessons that need to be carried beyond the recovery community to become a part of our whole culture.

Brenda Schell's remarks underscore why I had to write this book. The skills and techniques that facilitate recovery from an addiction can also provide self-improvement opportunities for anyone, addicted or not. That's what these pages are about.

SHEDDING LIGHT ON OUR DARKER NATURE

Those of us in recovery count our blessings and are grateful. We learn how to want what we have and this helps anchor us in the present time, which is crucial because, as research shows us, a wandering, restless mind is an unhappy mind.

Because you are reading this book, you either sense or have identified a need, an area of improvement you want to focus on. But remember, there is no quick fix, either in this book or in life. I've looked for all of the quick fixes and none of them worked as advertised. So, sorry, the quick fix is a myth.

This book isn't a fad diet, either; it's not some kind of self-help fantasy. But the lessons you will learn here can make life more tolerable. The principles in this book can help you have the fullest possible human experience.

A word of caution: Don't set yourself up for failure by attempting to do all ten lessons simultaneously and incorporate them into your life all at once. Try working on them one at a time. Try to picture the ten lessons as life skills found on a circle. They can be arranged randomly on the circle or in the order I present them. They naturally overlap; life is too messy to ever be compartmentalized. Together, the ten lessons are a process you enter anywhere on the circle, based on mere chance, your own nature and preferences, or your current circumstances. As you get into the process, the order of the lessons that works best for you will become clear.

Think of them as a new lifestyle; changes you will slowly implement for the rest of your time on this planet. This thought can be scary, but just keep reminding yourself, *There are no quick fixes; quick fixes don't exist.*

Consider this book an opportunity to investigate how your life is going. Ask yourself the following questions:

Am I generally content with the way things are?
Are my emotions mostly on an even keel?
Are my personal relationships strong and supportive?
Is there enough joy in my life?

Your answers may lead to the realization that what you need is recovery—a recovery that is unique, personal, and crucial for you. Recovery is about finding something we've lost, and what we have lost is our true self. Alienation from self is a byproduct of this culture of ours and its fixations, and we are all trying to find ourselves—whether we realize it or not. Addicts in recovery have discovered a process for achieving just that.

These pages give you the practical tools mastered and lived every day by those countless people who have successfully stayed in recovery. It may take some time to get off the Ferris wheel of repeating your mistakes over and over, but if you're going to be compulsive about something, you can't do much better than relentlessly pursuing a healthy lifestyle.

So consider this book a gift from the recovery community to all of humanity. Most of society continues to accept us addicts only reluctantly, not yet knowing what we have to give back. But what you now hold in your hands could, hopefully, change all that.

WHAT
ADDICTS
KNOW

FIND OUT WHO YOU ARE

Everything that irritates us about others can lead us to an
understanding about ourselves.

—CARL JUNG

Addicts in long-term recovery learn the importance of
finding out who they really are beneath all of the lies and
self-deception. That discovery of self is necessary if they
are to develop sufficient awareness to eventually find
contentment. Imagine the benefits to all of humanity if
more people uncovered their authentic selves and, as
a result, pursued a healthier, more honest standard for
well-being.

MEET PATTY POWERS, addictions recovery coach. Patty plays the role of mirror for her clients. By living with each of them for up to a month at a time in their own homes, she reflects back at them every day, and even moment to moment, how devious and manipulative the incessant inner dialogue of voices that distract them, delude them, sabotage them, and warp their personalities can be.

She has observed how the first transformation stage in addiction recovery comes from a self-awareness that develops, usually slowly, by practicing honesty and humility with self and others. Another necessary ingredient is self-acceptance of your "authentic" self, whatever that turns out to be. Addicts so rationalize their actions that they can't hear the truth or actually feel and express feelings unless something or someone penetrates and short-circuits their inner chatty dialogue of noise, fear, and denial.

One of Patty's clients, a woman with a very successful career whom we will call Nancy, hired Patty for a month to help her break a dependency on prescription drugs. She developed a problem with painkillers and antidepressants in the wake of the attacks of 9/11, and shortly thereafter had to cope with the painful aftermath of a difficult divorce.

Patty noticed early on that Nancy would begin feeling drowsy any time she began to feel stress. Not only was Nancy unaware of this pattern, she vehemently denied there was any connection between her fatigue and her unexpressed feelings. Nancy showed very little self-awareness, and that was sabotaging her attempts to maintain sobriety.

One of the advantages of having a full-time sobriety coach such as Patty, as opposed to being in a thirty-day rehab facility, is the constant personalized mirror for self-reflection that the sobriety coach holds up, coupled with the new life skills that clients learn and practice within the familiar world of their own living spaces. In recovery herself for several decades from heroin, Patty lives in New York City but has stayed with clients throughout the United States and in Britain and Canada. She has coached alcoholics and just about every other kind of drug addict known to medical science.

Whenever her client Nancy appeared fatigued despite having engaged in little or no physical exertion during the day, Patty would say to her, "Check in with yourself. What are you feeling right now?"

When Nancy seemed to be withdrawing, Patty would ask, "Where did you just go? What were you thinking about?"

Any time Patty caught Nancy future tripping—feeling unexpressed fear—she would instruct her, "Let's get you back in your body. Close your eyes and breathe deeply. Feel your feet, your legs, your entire body."

After several weeks of this often-annoying routine, Nancy finally began getting in the habit of bringing herself back to the present moment whenever the inner dialogue of her addict mind got out of control and tried to undermine her sobriety. Through this process she was rediscovering her authentic self.

Patty's constant vigilance, combined with her barrages of penetrating questions and the grounding exercises, gradually began to dispel all of Nancy's rationalizing stories until one day a significant breakthrough occurred. Nancy returned to her former home to pick up some belongings from her married days, and the visit triggered the release of a lifetime of feelings. She got tired and sleepy as soon as she walked through the door, and felt as if she stayed in the house for any length of time, she would have an over-powering urge to use drugs again.

"You were right!" Nancy later blurted to Patty. "I understand the connection now. I feel it. I see that I react to my feelings by wanting to check out with sleep."

Once addicts have that first revelatory glimpse of their true self hiding beneath all of the layers of drama and trauma, it's as if they are coming out of a sleepwalking trance. Consequently, they should keep repeating this mantra: "Don't go back to sleep! Never go back to sleep!" Without vigilance it's easy to slip back into an unconscious state. In Nancy's case, her revelation had a chain reaction that put into place all of the elements necessary for her sustained recovery.

Of course, many people who aren't addicts also suffering from loneliness, isolation, grief, fear, or whatever else afflicts the human spirit. They lead lives of quiet desperation. Having someone they can be themselves with, someone who they can be honest and self-revealing without fear of judgment with is, in my experience, an essential therapeutic first step to achieving wellness and healing. In this sense we all have the capacity—and, indeed, the duty—to become one another's sobriety and mental health coach, acting as mirrors reflecting one another's souls.

Too many people are sleepwalking through life, with no self-awareness. One symptom of our collective narcolepsy may be the periodic violent outbursts of shootings and mayhem that charac-terize our society. I am convinced that the lessons we take from the collective addiction and recovery experience can also tell us a lot about the mental health origins of gun violence in the United States, especially showing the common link between childhood trauma and its impact on the developing brain.

Addicts can lose just about everything in their lives and still sur-vive, "But people in broader society who experience real hardships don't have the experience or life skills to cope very well," said

Patty Powers. "The intensity of the fear and grief and financial stress since 9/11 and the Great Recession are all adding up. During the late 1920s and early '30s at the start of the Great Depression, guys jumped off buildings in response to losing everything in the stock market. They didn't shoot up their families and groups of strangers. The level of violence and addiction going on today is indicative of the huge pressure of stress from trauma that has built up in all areas of life. Addicts try to cope by getting high because they are afraid of being overwhelmed by their feelings. Getting in touch with our feelings in a healthy way can help us to stop killing ourselves and each other."

SELF-AWARENESS
UNMASKS YOUR AUTHENTIC SELF

Like most people entering recovery from an addiction, I was in a state of confusion for at least the first six months to a year, feeling as if I had been trapped in a hazy bubble that made it difficult to engage in any kind of reality other than brushing my teeth and getting dressed every day. In recovery, the word "mocus" is used to describe that haze. Early recovery is a basic survivalist kind of head space. Although self-awareness can and often does develop over time, "normies" too often think of people in recovery as being stuck in that twilight zone head space.

"By the time I recognized that I had a problem with alcohol, I was very confused about who I was and where I was going," Dan Duncan, the director of community services for the National Council on Alcoholism and Drug Abuse in St. Louis, told me, echoing a common refrain. "Self-awareness is integral to recovery because you lose your authentic self in addiction. Alcohol and drugs have a warping effect. Finding your way out is a gradual self-examination process. The joy of recovery for me was the adventure of self-discovery. I really wanted to know who the heck I was. Am I the guy who lied so much when I was drinking, or am I the decent guy buried underneath all of the crap? When I finally found out and rediscovered myself, my mother said to me, 'I finally have my son back.'" Today, Dan has more than three decades in recovery and works as director of community services in the St. Louis area for the National Council on Alcoholism and Drug Abuse, dedicating his life to helping others on the recovery path.

Self-awareness is the necessary first step to taking personal responsibility for your life. Self-awareness triggers the process of finding out who you really are so you can deal honestly with yourself and others. Self-awareness is a foundation for 12-Step recovery programs because it's an acknowledgment that whatever you have been doing hasn't been working for you.

Not everybody is interested in becoming self-aware, yet I believe that all addicts and alcoholics are seekers looking for answers to life's questions. Drug and alcohol abuse isn't just their way of self-medicating; it's also their attempt to attain some kind of greater consciousness. Unfortunately, using addictive substances to get there leads to a dead end.

Once in recovery, most people begin to explore who they really are, or who they really want to be, in order to solidify and sustain their recovery. You want to get rid of the triggers and the underlying causes and conditions that made you behave the way you did. That can be a thorny challenge for anyone, addict or not. "Most of what we do from childhood on is reacting to what happens to us," author and magazine journalist David Sheff explained to me. "We develop coping mechanisms and that takes us further away from who we are."

As you get deeper into recovery, you eventually feel compelled to ask, "What have I been doing with my life? I've lived a lie. I've lived in reaction my whole life. So who the hell am I?"

These questions are useful for non-addicts as well, of course. They are universal, but they take on a heightened sense of urgency among people dealing with recovery issues.

An important part of the Who Am I self-examination is reassessing the opinions and attitudes that underlay your decision-making. In my case, I had to ask myself questions like, *What color couch do I like?* I know this sounds trivial, but it's an example of a question that ultimately becomes revealing. People would ask me, "Do you like this couch?" And I would answer, "I don't know. Do you like it? Because if you like it, maybe I do, too." I didn't know enough about myself to even know what color couch I liked.

Developing self-awareness is about realizing something as basic as I don't even know what color couch I like. Some people might just leave it up to a professional or a friend to tell them what kind of couch they should like. Developing self-awareness is about realizing you don't even know something as basic about yourself as the colors you prefer.

Self-awareness is about a lot more than just having opinions. Opinions matter because you can latch onto them without necessarily having any visceral connections to them. An opinion is one thing, how you *feel* about something is entirely different. Addicts live in their heads most of the time. Recovery is about moving from your head to your heart. Self-awareness facilitates that.

If you like a couch because a parent liked it, or you saw it in a movie once, or the person you were dating at the time thought it was a cool couch, then you like that couch for superficial reasons. Recovery involves a deeper investigation into what really makes you tick. Do you like that couch just because you want to be a people pleaser? Once you get closer to your authentic self, you may realize you actually hate that damn couch and you aren't afraid to say so.

There are many layers to penetrate during recovery, and that's why it takes so much time. It's not an easy exploration of "I just want to find out what I really like." The trajectory of a person's life often obscures very diabolically who they really are, making self-awareness even more difficult to attain.

I had been so intoxicated and brainwashed by where I came from in life that I accepted a lot of what I wouldn't dream of accepting today. I came from a place where accomplishment and activity were highly valued, where just sitting around and connecting with someone was not. I came from a family where everything we did had to have a purpose, where there were strong convictions about giving back to society. Later in life, I came to realize much of that family behavior was really about getting recognition. Everybody was more or less out for themselves, as many human beings are, but it was especially magnified in my family.

Is that part of my authentic self? Yes, because that's where I came from, although I denied that out-for-myself part of my upbringing for many years because it was uncomfortable for me to behave that way. It's not uncomfortable for me to behave like that today, however. It's not a particularly attractive quality, but it is part of who I am at my core. Is it a part of my personality or my character that I would like to change? Yes. Just because you discover your authentic self doesn't mean it's necessarily good or that you like it or want to preserve it.

I like moving fast. I like sucking the marrow out of life. It's the family dynamic that I come from. Is it really me? I don't know, but I've accepted it as part of me and I like it. There was this sort of daredevil ethic I grew up with, trying to show who you were as a man. Driving or flying a plane with a broken foot or playing football while you were skiing on a mountain was the kind of stuff that was typical in my family. The more dangerous the stunts you pulled and the more you pushed the envelope, the more attention and admiration you got. That was never who I was, though at the time I wanted to be like that.

When we begin the process of trying to change, it's often difficult because the behavior instilled in us is so engraved that to do something differently feels wrong. It doesn't feel good. And addicts are addicted to feeling good. So if we're not feeling good, many of us just feel, "What the hell do I care?"

LIFE REWARDS AUTHENTICITY

Geoffrey S. Mason knew he needed help when he woke up in the south of France and didn't know where he was or what he had been doing the night before, although he knew it had something to do with an assignment covering a sporting event for ABC Sports. His increasingly heavy social drinking had stolen his identity and put him on a career treadmill that was undermining his reputation and self-esteem. So finally, in 1983, he checked himself into the Betty Ford Center.

Five years into recovery, Geoffrey had, in his words, "reclaimed my life and my career aspirations," and was named executive producer of ABC Sports, picking up twenty-six Emmy Awards during his career. "I wouldn't have had even a remote prayer for getting that job if I hadn't gotten sober," he said. "I wouldn't have had a remote prayer for a successful marriage before getting sober."

Only by getting in touch with his authentic self while in recovery, stripping away all the layers of self-deceit, was Geoffrey able to master the life skills necessary for a highly successful career and an eventual stable relationship leading to marriage. "Only when the poison in me was out of me could I know myself. There had been nothing real about my life. I was acting with artificiality. I didn't want to lie anymore. I learned who my true self was and I was okay with myself."

Most human beings want to feel special. They want to feel like they matter. They want to know that when they walk into a room, people care they are there. Therein is part of the genius of 12-Step programs. When you walk into one of those 12-Step meeting rooms, people really care that you are there and they show it.

When I first joined a 12-Step program, I thought I wanted to quit drinking and doing drugs and be a star like Tom Cruise. It took fifteen years for me to discover the real reason for me being there was to find my authentic self. A lot of people never get there. They are never able to turn their backs on who they are that doesn't work for them anymore. You gain tremendous freedom when you discard what doesn't work in your life.

The recovery journey is a long one. You're going to attain a different level of awareness and see stuff about yourself that you don't like and want to get rid of. The journey is about getting a clearer picture of your true self—your likes and dislikes, the traits that are genuine and those that are false, and what you will keep versus what needs to be discarded.

Part of finding and accepting the authentic self is getting to a point where you're not a victim anymore. You make conscious choices about what you want in your life and what you don't want. You realize, finally, it's up to you.

The reason why I don't drink or take drugs today is because I don't want to lose who I am. I would become less of Chris, and my commitment in recovery is to become *more* of me, not less. When you become more of you, the universe rewards you—you become happier and more successful, you have better relationships.

I'm willing to try almost anything. I'm always curious to see whether I'll like it and whether I'll want to do it again. If I go scuba diving and have a miserable time, I'm not going to go again just because I think it's cool to go scuba diving. If I go to yoga and it makes me feel good and I think it's good for me in terms of my health, I'm going to go every day regardless of what people think.

Much of my self-awareness has come from doing the deeper work. I've tried every kind of therapy imaginable. I've gone to workshops for relationships and for getting more in touch with the authentic self. A workshop called Sage and Warrior I did with my ex-wife was so powerful it brought us to our knees and had us crying on the floor. It wasn't abusive, everybody was safe, but the workshop was really hard emotionally. While there, I finally experienced living in my heart and not just in my head. I'm not talking about feeling love for somebody or feeling the presence of God. In this workshop I did actually move from my head to my heart. It was like nothing I've ever felt from a drug, love, sex, or anything else. It was the most profound, amazing experience of my life and lasted for about three weeks and then slowly faded away.

It might have been bliss. I felt as if I didn't filter anything through my mind. I was completely present and totally conscious, experiencing life directly through my heart. There was nothing there but me. So I do know something better is possible.

Attaining this awareness of an authentic self is about getting rid of the nonsense that doesn't serve you and diminishes your experience of life. That is what happens in 12-Step program meetings because what goes on in those meeting rooms is authentic and real, more real than most people ever experience in their lifetimes. But it's only the beginning.

Critical to the recovery process is realizing you aren't a victim in any part of your life, so you shouldn't blame anything or anyone but yourself for whatever happens in your life, be it good or bad. This is the essence of taking personal responsibility and being accountable for how you live your life.

I slip back into autopilot periodically, even when it comes to my self-awareness. Patterns and behaviors and beliefs are impressed upon us from an early age, so it's easy to return to them sometimes. As Gandhi framed the challenge for us—and I am paraphrasing—the man who changes himself is greater than the man who conquers ten thousand armies.

THE ROAD TO CONTENTMENT

Meditation has been an important tool in my self-transformation process because it brings me back to being in the moment. If I take the time to meditate, I get to go on pause.

Mindfulness techniques are as enormously useful to those in recovery as they are for "normies" who want better tools for navigating the pressures and chaos of daily life. These techniques facilitate the constant vigilance necessary to prevent relapse. If you mindfully pause before you respond or react, you can actually get more awareness in that brief interval.

The practices of meditation and yoga keep you in the present because of their focus on the breath. Yoga in particular got me through my battle with hepatitis C. Like meditation, yoga is about shutting off the mind. The quieter my mind is, the closer I am to my authentic self.

Before starting meditation and yoga I had no idea about breath or how important it is to health and well-being. If you're just focused on the postures, you're missing the point. The point is breath. Breath is everything. I used to smoke cigarettes and then cigars while in recovery. I cannot believe I did that, especially because of my awareness now about the importance of breath.

When I separated from my wife and kids and went through hepatitis C treatment, my acting career melted away. No Tom Cruise for me. All of that happened in about a year, and that is when I decided to write my first book. During that time, I attended yoga classes every day, meditated, and went to 12-Step meetings. I could have gotten drunk or even killed myself, which a lot of people do during hepatitis C treatment because it makes you feel utterly hopeless. Instead, thanks to the breath practices, this difficult experience strengthened my recovery. I said to myself, *Okay, this is razor's edge. I can drink or take drugs. I can kill somebody or kill myself. But that's not going to happen.* I made a conscious decision that this would be a transforming time for me.

During that dark period in my life I wrote my memoir, *Symptoms of Withdrawal.* It was cathartic and changed my whole life. I came away from that experience telling people that if you want to get closer to your authentic self, write your life story. I don't care whether you publish it or trash it. Even if you just call it journaling. If you take it on, you're going to find out a lot of revealing things about yourself.

When growing up, if you were a people pleaser, you may never have said what you really wanted or felt and always did what everybody wanted you to do. And you probably emerged a resentful and angry person. That anger has to come out somehow, someday. You don't have to have been an addict, of course, to be a people pleaser, or to be at the mercy of the people who socialized you. But I'm here to tell you that whether you're an addict or not, if you don't learn how to serve your authentic self, you're going to feel resentful, and this will affect all of the relationships in your life.

When people don't know themselves, they have few, if any, boundaries. They're confused, and it's hard for them to get any kind of clarity on anything. When you begin to set boundaries, however arbitrary they are, it gives you a foothold for making a statement about yourself. Boundary setting is a huge deal in realizing who you are. It gives you a heightened awareness of what's possible.

If you want to discover your authentic self, it's important for your self-growth to try a lot of different things and do so fearlessly. Also critical for self-awareness is understanding that you may have a tendency to engage in contempt before investigation. A lot of times people come into recovery with the attitude of, "Oh, I don't like that. No, I don't want to do that. I don't want to talk about that." They display contempt before investigating. For example, if you want to find out what you really like to eat, you've got to try a bunch of different foods. You can't just say "I don't like Thai food" if you've never really tried it. You've got to experiment and rid yourself of contempt and fear to ever discover who you are really capable of becoming.

Are the most authentic people, the ones most true to self, also among the happiest people? Not necessarily. But I do think the most authentic folks are the most centered, the most fearless, the most accepting. But are they happy? I think a more fitting word is "content."

Though self-awareness isn't necessarily synonymous with happiness, I believe that contentment is a possible outgrowth of self-awareness. Today, I know contentment. Are there still things that I'm not content with and want to change? Yes. I want to feel more peaceful and be less driven. Am I going to get around to that? Yes, but meanwhile I'm content.

If you're going down this self-exploratory path, you must accept that it's not going to be easy. You've got to be constantly vigilant to avoid slipping back into old toxic patterns of behavior. Whether you are in recovery from an addiction or not, the payoff is the promise of self-realization and contentment. The promise is *the real you*!

Dark Nights of the Soul

KRISTEN JOHNSTON is one of the most genuinely funny people I have ever known. She lights up every conversation with her disarming wit and candor. You may remember her as the two-time Emmy Award-winning actress in *3rd Rock from the Sun* and as an actress in two of the Austin Powers comedies. She also authored the addiction-recovery memoir *Guts: The Endless Follies and Tiny Triumphs of a Giant Disaster.* Here is what she had to say about the authenticity that can emerge from trauma and hardship:

"I'm convinced that the only people worth knowing are those who've had at least one dark night of the soul . . . Recovering addicts and alcoholics sometimes refer to this as their 'bottom,' but it happens to almost everyone, at some point or another. It's that life-changing moment when everything you've always wanted to become, everything you actually are, and everything you know you'll never be, all slam into each other with the deadly force of three high-speed trains. It's the night of your reckoning, the terrifying moment when your mask falls away and you're forced to see what's actually been festering underneath it all these years. You finally see who you *really are,* instead of who you've always *pretended* to be."

PET PEEVES, FINGER POINTING,
AND YOUR "SHADOW"

Self-awareness also involves learning about the "shadow" side of your nature, those unconscious aspects of self that influence behaviors and beliefs, yet remain mostly hidden. The late

Dr. W. Brugh Joy, author of *Avalanche: Heretical Reflections on the Dark and the Light,* a book about excavating those hidden aspects, your shadow material, conducted Dark Side Conferences across the United States. One exercise in the meetings involved "the pointing finger," an examination of what pointing your finger at someone or something reveals about your own judgment or defensiveness, your true self. (As we say in recovery, if you point a finger there are three fingers pointing back at you.)

"Pet peeves are wonderful ways to catch the shadow because the pet peeve is actually the key to something about you," said Dr. Joy.

This is a delicious exercise: Criticize an individual, work on expressing everything—just unleash all of it—no tiptoeing around, no modulating the energy—just get in touch with these forces and get them out, let them out fully.

Then begins the process of re-weaving the forces back into your own nature. You point your finger, but then you begin to see that there is a pattern to it, that it has shown up in your life from time to time as well, this very same thing. Not the same person doing the exact same thing, but you begin to read the pattern. Is it abandonment, or is it a rejection mystery, is it martyrdom? There are various kinds of patterns that you'll see. Then you trace it back as far as you can go in your own life, where other circumstances had exactly the same kind of patterning to it.

(For more about Lesson #1, including the results of several research studies, visit our website, www.Recover2Live.com.)

LESSON #1: PARTING SHOT

Stop what you're doing right now (reading this book) and ask yourself the following simple questions. Some will be more relevant to you than others. All should make you think—and that's exactly the idea:

- Do you like what you see when you look in the mirror? Do you smile at yourself?
- What are your two best qualities?
- What are two of your personality traits you don't like?
- Would you want to be your friend?

There are no right or wrong answers, of course. Just *your* answers. Socrates' advice resonates down through the centuries: Know thyself. Introspective questions like these help you do just that.

LESSON #2

ACCEPT PERSONAL RESPONSIBILITY

> The willingness to accept responsibility for one's own life is the source from which self-respect springs.
>
> —JOAN DIDION

People in recovery from addictions must take responsibility for their own actions and eventual wellness. Imagine how much more harmonious and healthy all human interactions would be if everyone stopped playing the blame game and the role of victim.

MEET JACK GRISHAM. As Jack's father lay dying in a San Diego naval hospital following a heart attack, he looked up into his son's eyes and mumbled, "I love you." It was only the second time in twenty-three-year-old Jack's life that he had ever heard his father say those words.

Not knowing how to respond, Jack replied with the only thing he could think of that might make his father happy: "I'll go home and mow the lawn."

The next day his father died, and Jack immediately bagged up all of his father's clothing and other belongings and threw them into Dumpsters.

Not long afterward, Jack's mother filed a lawsuit alleging that her husband had died prematurely from the stress induced by the demands of his shipping industry job. The employer fired back with legal documents arguing that the elder Grisham's stress was due entirely to his son Jack, whose outrageous troublemaking had constantly weighed on Grisham.

There could be no doubt that Jack had caused his parents considerable grief. Jack's mother affirmed that when she confessed to him years later, "Not a night went by that I wasn't praying you wouldn't get killed."

Alone among the family's five children, Jack had been arrested— taken into custody at least two dozen times, in fact—on charges ranging from vandalism and assault, to throwing a brick through a cop car window and incitement to riot. As the lead singer for a notorious West Coast punk rock band, Jack defiantly called himself an anarchist. He considered violence, drug use, and debauchery badges of honor. He painted his face pasty white, wore cowboy boots with sharpened spurs, and generally acted like a maniac during his band's punk rock performances. He intentionally cultivated an aura of glowering menace.

Through all of the years of senseless mayhem, including having their home shot at and his car firebombed, Jack's parents had stood by him, if only passively. They never kicked him out of the house. To this day, Jack marvels at that, though part of the reason may have been his father's paralyzing alcoholism, which rendered the family dysfunctional on many different levels.

Within a year of his father's death, Jack began trying to get sober from his drug and alcohol dependencies. He had simply grown tired of being out of control, and he had a girlfriend nursing a serious drug problem of her own. He wanted to get sober with her. Given the rampant drug abuse within the music circles he traveled, getting sober was a radical thing to do. Instead of thumbing his nose at government and other institutions of society, as his song lyrics so frequently did, he was now rejecting a central lifestyle tenet of the subculture within which he had become a role model. His friends thought he had either gone crazy or was pulling yet another prank on everyone.

His sobriety came in fits and starts. His wife, the girl he had gotten sober with, relapsed and left him, but he continued going to 12-Step meetings. Jack finally broke free of drugs and alcohol for good on January 8, 1989. He has been sober ever since.

"For me, when I got sober, it was like a tidal wave had come and I was swept along with it," he explained to me several decades into his recovery.

I'm not really seeing what's happening, and the tidal wave dropped me off, and as the water recedes, I start to see things. Like, I'm in my twenties and living with my mother. The water sucks back some more. I've got a daughter I haven't been seeing. It sucks back some more. I am being blamed for my father's death. It keeps receding, more and more, and I am able to see all of the damage my behavior has caused. It was like a coroner's blanket being pulled back slowly from over a frightening mess. I had started to wake up, and my head began to clear.

Though some people tried to convince Jack it wasn't his fault his father had died at age fifty-five, Jack wasn't buying it. He said:

I got the full realization of what I had done to my father. I saw my role in his death. I had to accept my role, take responsibility, and stop playing the victim. My sobriety demanded it. Justice demanded it. I couldn't blame anything anymore, not my anger, not my behavior, not my father's alcoholism, not on our screwed-up society, not on police brutality, not on an untrustworthy government—not on any of the other targets I used to sing about on stage with my band. I realized how I had created all of the negativity I was wallowing in, and my own selfishness had created my own demons.

Not long into recovery Jack visited his father's grave for the first time since the burial. He stood there alone, a stream of painful memories washing over him, and had the longest conversation of his life with his father. "I told him how sorry I was. I told him how I had hurt him and added to his stress and pain. I told him how I had changed. I was in recovery. I had a bright future ahead of me. I told him I hoped he could be proud of me now."

With recovery, Jack was reborn into another way of thinking. *He took responsibility for all parts of his life.* He became a new kind of role model. He still plays music, but without any of the other lifestyle toxins and attachments from his previous life. He has become a clinical hypnotherapist and an inspirational speaker performing on a new stage—before hundreds of people at a time—extolling the life-changing miracles of recovery from addiction.

WHAT MAKING AMENDS DOES

When someone goes into recovery from an addiction, that person should take an inventory of who they really are. Everyone on the planet could benefit from doing this periodically, regardless of whether they are in recovery from an addiction or not, because that examination prepares you for a journey down the road of self-transformation toward becoming a more contented person.

This self-examination involves compiling a detailed checklist, much like what retail stores do in their annual inventory of merchandise, so you know what resources are available to you and what is missing. First, you must identify and understand the primary problem in your life, which could be just about anything, not just an addiction. Second, you need to develop an understanding of your responsibility in having created that problem. Third, accept that you're responsible for changing the mind-set and behaviors that initiated or accompany the problems you experience.

Part of that process, the accepting personal responsibility piece, involves a realization that you're responsible for virtually everything that happens in your life. You can't legitimately claim victimhood. And you are the one who must fix the problems in your life—you can't pawn off that responsibility. You must hold yourself accountable for your words and deeds.

Beginning in the 1970s, this theme struck a responsive chord with the more than one million people who participated in awareness training programs and workshops pioneered by groups such as est (Erhard Seminars Training), Landmark Forum, Lifespring, Temenos, and Pathways. These programs were designed to expand conscious awareness—bringing darkness into light—and improve the way people experience themselves and one another.

During these workshops, ground rules—stringently enforced—emphasized personal accountability, including something as simple as promising to be on time for each session. That might seem trivial, but punctuality (or lack of it) reveals a lot about people's reliability. In many of these programs, if you were late to sessions or back from breaks, you were given the opportunity to stand up in front of everyone and confess that you had no one to blame but yourself. Excuses sound extremely lame when someone has to publicly confront an audience of faces staring back, like a giant mirror of self-reflection.

Early in my recovery, I blamed my upbringing for my having developed a drug dependency. I actually believed I was victimized on a variety of levels, and I felt totally justified in feeling and voicing that victimization. It's true that I grew up in a family plagued by codependency, and I wasn't taught very good interpersonal skills from my parents. They were both alcoholics, and my mother was devastated by the tragic events in her life, including losing two of her brothers to assassins. She became withdrawn and emotionally unavailable. People around me would get mad, and they couldn't talk about it because they were afraid of their own anger. So they hid away all of this resentment and anger and plastered a smiley face on top of it. In our family, we would hide our feelings of victimization behind a mask of stoicism, which meant we couldn't talk about any of it or deal with it on any level.

As with many people in recovery, I've struggled with an inability to get along with other people, whether it's my kids, my family, or in my love life. I could be in a loving relationship, but then get suspicious, thinking the person was only in my life to get something. She didn't really love me for me. She just loved where I had come from, the family I grew up with, or the possessions I had. She's using me—that was my greatest fear.

Where did this message come from, and was it true? What was my responsibility insofar as dealing with it? I came to realize it wasn't something being done to me. It was something I had created, and I had to take responsibility for it. Why did I create it? One reason has to do with self-worth. I did get a lot of attention for who I was in my life—the famous family I came from—and I became somewhat wedded to that image. In some ways, it was my only measure of my own self-worth.

During recovery, I slowly began to see my part in everything that happens to me. I no longer pretend to be a victim. So now when I'm in a good relationship and those whispers begin in my mind—"Maybe she's not really here for *you*. Maybe she's just really good at hiding her *real* intentions"—I recognize those inner voices as my fears resurfacing, as the feelings of insecurity that make me wonder whether or not I'm good enough for her and if she's going to leave me.

Once I developed the understanding that I'm just manufacturing those fears, I had a choice and I could do something about it. When the inner voices try to sabotage me, I can call upon recovery skills and resources to counteract them and defuse their emotional impact.

Taking responsibility for thoughts and actions is a process. At every step you need to ask yourself what is real and what is merely your projection based on fear, habits, and upbringing. Most people don't believe they have the time to work through this process. They're running as fast as they can just to survive. Admittedly, it does take some time and energy to develop the capability and desire to do it. You need the willingness to engage yourself. It has to become important to you. That is true for everyone, but for addicts it's absolutely crucial because for them it's really a life and death issue.

LEVELS OF PERSONAL RESPONSIBILITY

During my recovery from drug addiction, I've gotten to know dozens of experts in the recovery field. One of them, a well-known addictions-recovery specialist in New York, began an entire branch of research in 1998 to study the various approaches people use to stay in recovery from drugs and alcohol. Many of her close friends are in drug and alcohol recovery, and she has interviewed countless others in recovery, giving her a unique, valuable point of view.

"I've grown as a human being by accepting and acknowledging personal responsibility, and that's happened as a result of being in contact with people working on themselves," she told me.

When I began in recovery research, I interviewed people and heard their recovery stories and saw what they were going through in working the Twelve Steps. That experience taught me an enormous amount of what it means to be a human being. I am a "normie" but have grown enormously from learning these lessons, which can benefit everyone.

In looking back on their lives, many people insist on blaming others; they have to feel like victims. This blaming tendency goes back to childhood. We don't usually teach children that all actions have consequences. For some reason in this society, saying I'm sorry or I was wrong feels so horrible that many people would rather not. It's easier to blame what happens on someone else than to say you were wrong. I know many people whose lives haven't turned out the way they wanted, and they blame it on circumstances or someone else. In any situation involving someone else, they had a role to play, even if it was just a small role. So it's always best for us to ask ourselves if there is anything we would and could have done differently, and if so, would that have changed the outcome. Look at *your* role in every situation. That is what personal responsibility is really about.

Is it possible to maintain recovery from an addiction without embracing personal responsibility? Many specialists don't believe so, and I agree. People cannot improve their lives without realizing that they have a part to play in the outcome. One psychologist explained:

People are often afraid of change and so they stay in less-than-satisfying situations because it's easier than making a change. But if you are self-aware, you can start acknowledging that there are things you can do that empower you and allow you to put yourself in the driver's seat of your life. A lot of people say recovery to them is a second chance to become the person they wanted to be before addiction took their life away. They had to shed their moral code in order to survive as an addict. A successful addict has to lie, cover-up, and deceive. To be in active recovery, you have to rediscover the practice of a moral code and that includes the lesson of accepting personal responsibility.

WHAT EVERYONE CAN LEARN

You have to know who you are and who you aren't, and you need to cultivate an idea of who you want to become—all grounded in a foundation of personal responsibility—if you hope to achieve some level of contentment within your life.

"What people in broader society don't yet understand about people in recovery," explained Dan Duncan of the St. Louis-area National Council on Alcoholism and Drug Abuse, "is that those in recovery have taken responsibility for their illness. Recovery means you take responsibility for your own wellness. For general society there is a lesson in that because too often, as human beings, we get stuck in life, with depression or anxiety or lack of ambition. And then we say, 'Oh well, this is the way I am.' That is a huge cop-out. Those in recovery know the addiction is not who they are or want to be."

I think every human being has a desire to attain a higher self, to be a better person in every way possible. Yet society too often rewards people who aren't searching for the higher self. Take, for example, the abundant cases from Wall Street, Washington, DC, and Hollywood. Those cultures reward people who are looking out for themselves. Cutthroat behaviors and attitudes are effective and become the norm.

When I first got to Hollywood a friend of mine said, "The ethic here is not that you succeed. It's that you have to succeed and your best friend has to fail." The people who dominate Wall Street, Washington, DC, and Hollywood aren't necessarily sociopaths, but many of them have little concern about their actions and their actions' impact on others. Such people seem incapable of holding themselves accountable.

You may be reading this and thinking, *What does this have to do with me? I don't have any of these problems.* What I am saying is that we addicts have had to change ourselves and we've had to embrace spiritual principles to try to find our higher selves. It's a matter of survival for us. We've had to own what happens to us and take responsibility for our thoughts and actions. It may not be that much of a life and death issue right now for a non-addict but it's still an important path to greater well-being. And to get there, you'll have to have the courage to embrace these recovery principles.

What we learn as addicts in recovery is that if we focus on ourselves and we change ourselves according to spiritual principles, then we get along better with other people and, as a result, our little part of the world is a better place. It's that simple—yet it means everything.

PERSONAL RESPONSIBILITY
INVOLVES FORGIVENESS

Many people forgive others for transgressions simply so they can move on and aren't stuck in the past. "Without forgiveness we remain locked in a jail cell of past hurt and pain," wrote psychotherapist Donald Altman in his book *The Joy Compass: Eight Ways to Find Lasting Happiness, Gratitude, and Optimism in the Present Moment,* "all the while missing out on one of life's greatest learning opportunities. Consider that when you sit in that cell, you have labeled yourself as a victim and thrown away the key. Holding on to resentment, anger, and bitterness may provide some sense of vindication, justification, and solace, but it does not offer any hope of joy."

Joy and contentment are states of being we all seek in life, yet something we only see more clearly once we strip away materialistic pretensions and unrealistic expectations. The act of offering forgiveness to ourselves and others provides a time-tested way of transcending life's accumulated sufferings. This isn't a new idea, of course. Ancient wisdom enshrined the practice of forgiveness as part of a foundation for leading a spiritual life. But its relevance hasn't in any way diminished over the centuries.

In the 2,500-year-old Buddhist meditation known as "loving-kindness," a statement of forgiveness is the first blessing offered. Forgiveness is extended to anyone who may have harmed us, forgiveness is requested from anyone we may have harmed, and then forgiveness is offered back to us for any harm we have done to our own selves. That harm to self usually comes from the incessant sniping of our inner critic.

Our inner critic is that mental voice (or voices) that whispers or sometimes even screams at us with instructions about how we should feel and behave. We are told we aren't good enough, we're not deserving, we should always be right, we should never forget past wrongs, or we shouldn't trust anyone or anything—especially when it comes to giving or receiving love.

Taking a daily inventory of yourself and your thoughts—and in the process, raising your self-awareness—will help you identify that inner critic and begin to diminish its power over you. As Altman observed in his book, "Know that it will take time and practice to let go of old critical scripts or behaviors. Letting go is a first step. Remember to offer forgiveness to yourself when the critic reappears. Then, let go again. It takes time to rewire your brain for joy."

Keep in mind the practice of forgiveness isn't just about becoming a more spiritual, ethical, or better human being. During the past decade a large body of scientific research has documented the myriad ways the act of forgiving can directly enhance your physical and mental health.

One specialist described for me research in behavior medicine showing that people with spinal cord injuries who continued to blame themselves for the accident that caused the injuries didn't do well physically or mentally. "There is a significant association between your level of psychological and medical functioning and the act of blaming oneself," she said. "I did my dissertation on that. I interviewed people after an accident that had caused significant orthopedic injury, then six weeks or so later I asked them about their responsibility for the accident and for their healing. In the immediate aftermath, the person didn't take responsibility for the accident and injury. But there is a process whereby the person starts feeling responsibility for both the accident and their healing. Assuming personal responsibility allows them to maintain some element of control."

What Forgiveness Is and Is Not

FORGIVENESS IS a process, not some sudden lightning bolt of awareness. In his workshops, Herb Kaighan, a chemical dependency treatment expert, teaches such a process and starts with useful definitions of what forgiveness is and is not.

Forgiveness is *not*

- condoning,
- forgetting,
- tolerating,
- ignoring,
- approving,
- excusing,
- minimizing,
- pardoning,
- denying,
- absolving,
- reconciling,
- inviting to hurt again, or
- surrendering justice.

cont'd. on next page

cont'd. from previous page

Forgiveness *is* a decision to not

- retaliate,
- exact revenge,
- seek compensation, or
- judge.

Forgiveness *is* a decision to

- release them,
- release ourselves, and
- be released.

AN EXERCISE: GIVE YOURSELF
AND OTHERS LOVING KINDNESS

Words have healing powers if you let them truly affect you. There is an emotional hurt when someone harshly criticizes us and a blissful euphoria when someone lavishly praises us.

Try this little exercise. It's a mantra, a series of words intended to be used in prayer, meditation, or repeated as an invocation. I've adapted it from many sources, primarily Buddhist, although it's not religious dogma. Its repetition is a way to reprogram your thinking and emotional patterns so you naturally, and more readily, feel forgiving of yourself and others.

Either while sitting quietly with eyes closed, or even while going about your normal day, repeat these phrases over and over, mentally or out loud:

Allow me to forgive myself for hurting others.
Allow others to forgive me for hurting them.

Allow me to forgive me for hurting myself.
Allow my thoughts, words, and actions to always express
compassion and kindness toward all living beings.

———————

(For more about Lesson #2, including the results of several research
studies, visit our website, www.Recover2Live.com.)

LESSON #2: PARTING SHOT

Whose fault is it that you are who you are? That you do what you do? That you're not what you could be, should be, would be? Your parents'? A sibling's? A partner's? Society's? Or is it yours—your fault—at least partially?

OK, you can't control or change any of those other people. The only one you can affect is you. So take it on. Shoulder the burden. Take responsibility. No one else has to give a damn about you. Only *you* do. So accept it. Accept yourself. And the next time something goes wrong (as it surely will), don't look for someone or something to blame. Instead, look to yourself, do your best to make the situation better, and then move on.

LESSON #3

VISUALIZE THE LIFE YOU WANT

Our destination is never a place, but rather a new way of
looking at things.

—HENRY MILLER

People in recovery from addictions must forge a new
conception of self (or recover their authentic selves) in
order to get sober. Imagine if greater numbers of people
pursued their dreams by transforming themselves into
more positive, supportive, and grateful human beings.

MEET PENNY VIZCARRA. When Penny was three years sober, working a low-paying job in the medical field and struggling to support two children, she felt like she was going nowhere fast. One night she got a call from a 12-Step program friend who invited her and the kids out for pizza, which was good timing since impoverished Penny had absolutely nothing to feed her children that evening.

During the meal this man offered her some advice. He told her to visualize the life she wanted and do an affirmation to support that vision. The affirmation this man told Penny to use every day was simple and direct: "I am affluent and money comes to me."

If you think about it, saying something like that over and over every day can't help but be a confidence builder. Whether or not you believe that affirmations "magnetize" and draw to you what you want, you have to concede that it doesn't hurt to project an air of confidence and faith about reaching your goal.

What Penny visualized was a life that supported her children and made them happy. That was her focus and her motivating impulse. The vision she held for herself and her children had detail and clarity—she'd work for a movie studio, drive a certain car, and live in a certain neighborhood.

Pain is a touchstone to growth, as the saying goes, and Penny was scared enough and desperate enough that she embraced the affirmation like a thirsty desert traveler who has found an oasis.

What happened to her life in a matter of months is truly remarkable. The affirmation morphed into her reality. Her career became meteoric.

Six months after she began the affirmation, she was driving the Mercedes she had visualized, living in the neighborhood she had visualized for her children, and working at 20th Century Fox as a creative executive involved in the marketing campaigns for such hit films as *True Lies*.

"If you have the right motives you can actualize your visualization," Penny explained to me. "Not only do we create our own reality, if we ask God, He will show up to help us become who we want to be. By asking God to guide my life I feel very blessed to love what I do. I get up every day and ask God to keep me sober for that day, and I thank God every night for keeping me sober. I am a huge believer that when something I perceive as negative happens in my life, it will turn into a blessing."

YOU WILL UNDERESTIMATE
THE RESULTS OF CHANGE

When I first got clean and sober, one of my mentors told me I should make a list of what I wanted in my life. "You are sure to shortchange yourself because what you get will be far greater than what you put down," he predicted. I didn't really believe him at the time, but he turned out to be right.

Want to know why over the coming years you probably won't become the person you hope or expect to be? It's probably not for the reasons you think. Research psychologists report that it's because we humans are wired to underestimate—that's right, underestimate—rather than overestimate, how much we will change in the future.

That our tastes and preferences and opinions and personalities change with age, sometimes radically, is something we rarely take into account when we try to visualize the kind of life we want to have as we age. Social science researchers label this self-perception blindfold as "the end of history illusion."

In a study of more than nineteen thousand people who ranged in age from eighteen to sixty-eight, Harvard University psychologists put participants through a battery of tests that revealed the subjects' past and present favorite musical groups, foods, hobbies, and other life preferences. The test subjects were then asked their predictions of what their preferences would be in the future.[3] Years later, a clear pattern had emerged from the answers, a pattern consistent for all the study's age groups. Virtually everyone was much more skilled (and accurate) at recalling who they were in the previous decade of their lives than they were in predicting how much they would change over the next decade. In fact, the discrepancy between past and future perceptions was dramatic.

One of the Harvard researchers explained in the *New York Times* why this phenomenon occurs: "Believing that we just reached the peak of our personal evolution makes us feel good. The 'I wish that I knew then what I know now' experience might give us a sense of satisfaction and meaning, whereas realizing how transient our preferences and values are might lead us to doubt every decision and generate anxiety." In short, we don't know ourselves nearly as well as we might think we do.

This phenomenon works in practice when we cling to the present by imagining, for example, that we will always love loud disco music, or chicken fried steak smothered in gravy, or that huge tattoo with our first love's name burned into our left buttock.

---

3 Jordi Quoidbach et al., "The End of History Illusion," *Science* 339 (Jan 2013): 96–8, doi:10.1126/science.1229294.

Then we look back years later at our fleeting whimsies and feel regretful, embarrassed, and even superior to the immature fool we had been.

What we really think we want in life is always subject to change. None of us has a crystal ball, so we base our vision of a possible future and its options on what we know about the present. This often results in what social scientists call "miswanting," because our wants, like any other prediction about our future, are subject to error and change. "Although we tend to think of unhappiness as something that happens to us when we do not get what we want," wrote psychologists Daniel Gilbert and Timothy Wilson in 2000, "much unhappiness has less to do with not getting what we want and more to do with not wanting what we like. When wanting and liking are uncoordinated in this way one can say that a person has *miswanted*."[4]

So we may get what we want and not like what we get. Who hasn't experienced that? Our world is heavily populated by people who are struggling to be a person they ultimately aren't, pursuing wants and goals they ultimately won't like. It's no wonder that as a result, so many feel discontented and think life is meaningless. The tragedy is that most will never discover this fact of life until trauma or addiction drags them to rock bottom.

MANIFESTING THE NEW YOU

There's a practical side to spending one's life oblivious to your own untapped potential. Realistically, you can't constantly be looking for what you should do or who you are when you are

---

4 Daniel T. Gilbert and Timothy D. Wilson, "Miswanting: Some problems in the forecasting of future affective states," *Feeling and Thinking: The Role of Affect in Social Cognition,* (New York, NY: Cambridge University Press, 2000), pp. 178–97.

constantly consumed by work obligations, family responsibilities, and the myriad unpredictable travails and heartaches of human existence.

Searching for your true self and true calling in life can go on even when you're doing what you flat-out have to do—all those responsibilities and obligations. Because you're human, you find the time for self-examination, for worrying, for dreaming. You ponder what could be, what should be, and . . . sometimes sadly . . . what might have been. But then you concentrate on what's next. You look forward. And you start to ask yourself, *Can I do all of these things in total, or must I do them incrementally?*

Let's focus first on what you want your work life to look like. You want to be fulfilled, you want to be proactive and productive, you want to get paid well and be recognized for the work you do, and you want balance in your life. Many people will say, "This is totally unrealistic because it's not the way the world works." I would argue that it *does* work that way for people who take the time to figure some of this stuff out and who practice some of the techniques that Penny Vizcarra and others have used to actually get what they want.

Time and our perception of it may be the crux of the problem. Collectively, we humans have evolved conceptual machinery and a way of doing business that demands conformity. By contrast, what I am talking about here is a kind of nonconforming. It's having the courage *not* to conform, which is scary for many people.

There are many different ways to go about it. My son had two really good jobs but quit them both because he wasn't feeling fulfilled. It wasn't who he was. In the aftermath, he had a hard time finding a job that fit him, but I would argue that the process of being challenged to find a job is going to give him satisfaction he never would have had and lead him to places he would never have gone if he had just stayed on a gravy train.

It is an act of faith. It's also about keeping the focus on you and what you want and not thinking about how the machinery of the world works.

Some of you may have read that old but timeless book *Think and Grow Rich* by Napoleon Hill. It was one of the first books about manifesting your goals and desires. A lot of people get into manifesting and think, *I have to be specific and I have to make it happen on a daily basis.* But that approach, according to Hill and other people I respect who have done this work, is not necessarily true (although Penny Vizcarra certainly did it by envisioning the life she wanted for her children).

There is a belief that the universe has an energy that responds in kind to energy from consciousness. You attract what you put out there. So if you're full of negativity and fear and haunted by the "should haves" and "could haves" in your life, that's what you're going to get back. If you have the capacity to break out of those straitjackets and get excited about the possibilities in life, and you do the necessary things to manifest those possibilities, you aren't just wishing and praying for a desirable outcome. You are manifesting a new reality for yourself.

You may want to be rich or win the lottery or have wealth in your life. But you still have to ask yourself the following questions: How do I want my life to look when I have that? Do I want to give wealth away? What will my relationships look like? Am I asking for wealth for the right reasons?

The thing about wealth, somebody once said to me, is that you'll never know how miserable you can be until your ship finally comes in. You realize for the first time how material wealth is not the be-all and end-all. Not that wealth is a bad thing or making money is a bad thing. It's just that money in and of itself isn't going to give you contentment if you don't have balance in the other aspects of your life.

Imagine what is possible in your life, even if you can't bring yourself to believe it. The first step necessary is to overcome disbelief. (But be certain that what you imagine is possible and able to be orchestrated into reality.) Then consistently visualize the details of what this new life will look like and show up every day with energy and belief and enthusiasm, with the knowledge that it is your feelings of certitude that will draw it all to you.

Florence Griffith-Joyner was once the fastest woman in the world. Her nickname was Flo-Jo. I read an interview with her where she was asked, "How did you become the world's fastest woman?" She replied, and I am paraphrasing, "One day I thought, *I want to be the fastest woman in the world.* I had no idea how I was going to do that. I had no idea if it was possible. I just had a strong instinct toward it and I trusted that it was possible. I showed up every day with the energy to do whatever I had to do to make it happen."

To Flo-Jo, her goal was a point on the horizon. She had no idea how she was going to get there, but she trusted that a Higher Power, hard work, and her own internal guidance system would direct her to the destination. It became all about harnessing her talent to create a new reality for herself. That is fundamentally what I am talking about here for you and your life.

If you told me a decade ago that I would write a book about my life (*Symptoms of Withdrawal*) and it would bring me into a public role, advocating for recovery from the disease of addiction, I would have bet everything you were wrong. It just wasn't in my frame of reference. So we really have no idea how the energy of the universe, or what I would call its underlying spiritual energy, is going to actually manifest itself in our lives. It may, in fact, surprise us—in a delightful way.

I became an actor when I was thirty, right after I got sober. I got into acting for all the wrong reasons—primarily because I wanted to be famous and get paid a lot of money for doing very little work. I also didn't know what else I could do with my life at that time. My father had been an actor, of course, but when I first started acting, I didn't have a real attachment to the profession. There was nothing at my core that compelled me to act. It wasn't my true calling, but soon I developed an appreciation for the art of it and the effort it takes.

My whole life changed because I decided to write a book. My acting career was going nowhere, and I needed to do something else so I began to write. I now give speeches in front of hundreds of people. I'm an advocate. I do all this stuff, and it's effortless for me. I really believe I'm good at it. But out of nowhere, the universe let me use all of my talents—my acting ability, my legal background, my writing capability, my public speaking skills, all of it—and concentrate them into one useful, important, public service role.

A lot of people get stuck, and few envision or stumble into their true calling at an early age. Most of us find it through trial and error. Some people never find a role that fits who they are, if only because they never find their authentic self. "You cannot project the life you want without coming to grips with who you are," said William L. White, the emeritus senior research consultant at Chestnut Health Systems in Florida. That's one reason why the ten lessons in this book are ordered the way they are. Even though you don't necessarily have to proceed through them in sequence, there is a logical progression of development that could help you best recognize and realize the new you.

USE YOUR FEELINGS TO POINT THE WAY

When most people think of "visualizing" a goal or "visualization," they imagine a process where they "see" what they want in their future life and either write that down or create visual images from photos or drawings to represent that goal.

Clay Tatum, a successful home builder and entrepreneur I know in Santa Monica, has twenty-six years of sobriety, and he puts a different spin on his approach to a visualization practice. He has become adept at using his feelings to attract more of what he wants in life.

Here is how it works:

What I found is that my emotions are a guidance system and act as an indicator of what I'm thinking about. I track daily how I feel, which is where recovering people have an advantage, because we are very aware of our feelings. Because I am aware, I can tell—based on my feelings—which direction I'm looking in life. I can't monitor every thought, but I can be constantly aware of how I feel. When I feel good, I attract more things to my life to feel good about. That is the law of attraction in practice.

When you first start visualizing what you want in your life, the low-hanging fruit are things like financial security, loving relationships, beauty, health. People might call all that a get-rich scheme. Feeling abundance of joy, not abundance of material wealth, is the worthier and more effective goal. When I began to feel grateful for what I had in my life, I attracted more of it, including a very successful business, a wife I am madly in love with, four children. If you had asked me when I was newly sober, or had described my current circumstances, I might have said no thank you. What you couldn't have predicted for me is how I would feel at this stage of my life. It's taken me years in recovery to step back and see the canvas of my life and see that everything happened in terms of a change of my perception. I let go of old ideas. The keys to the kingdom are focusing exclusively on what is good in your life and what you want more of.

The first thing I did was limit negative input. A complaint is a type of affirmation, although it's a negative one that we say out loud. We have a feeling about it, we say it to others, but it just attracts more of the negative. Shift to a compliment instead of a complaint. You make a conscious choice to shift. We aren't powerless over our thoughts. We can choose the thoughts we want to focus on. I had to stop gossiping and being around gossips. I had to limit negative news, anything feeding my consciousness with negative input. I believe that positive prayer and affirmations are effective, and I practice that. Like most people in recovery, I am predisposed to a negative outlook, so I have to manufacture gratitude. I make gratitude lists a lot. My prayer is an affirmation of things going well in my life. I visualize through a vision board I make on my iPad, creating things I want and focusing on the good. I create a feeling state of joy by regularly doing that.

For normies, the folks not participating in 12-Step programs, Clay recommends starting the visualization process by acknowledging all of the things in your life you currently feel grateful for:

Make a list of your accomplishments, fifty of them. You have a driver's license, you graduated from high school. These seem like simple things, but a lot of people haven't achieved even those. So write it all down just to get some context about what you can feel grateful for. As you do this, your gratitude list grows. When you think about or visualize each accomplishment, summon a physical feeling of gratitude. The affirmation for you then becomes being more aware of what you want to be grateful for. When you put that out there, a shift in perception occurs. The more you start to feel that gratitude, having a negative or fearful thought becomes the exception, not the rule. Your positive feelings attract more positive feelings, and that attracts abundance until people are coming up to you and saying, "Man, you've got a great life going."

FIND YOUR DIRECTIONAL HERO

You've probably heard that heroes are made, not born. I kind of think it's both. Call it karma or whatever, but some people just seem destined to grow up and be an inspiration to millions of people, while others fall into the hero role simply by showing up with the right intentions and actions when they are most needed.

If you identify Gandhi or Einstein as your hero, it doesn't mean you are necessarily interested in nonviolent social change and advocacy or in physics. Both of these people spoke to the human condition and to the spiritual nature of it. They had the kind of life and championed the kind of principles that you might want to emulate.

Gandhi is my hero not for what he did in getting the British out of India and doing so with a philosophy of action based on nonviolence, although I certainly appreciate that. It's more about his experience of wrestling with his inner self that is most heroic to me.

The process of finding a hero is to begin thinking about who is heroic to you and all of the reasons why. We're talking about a living person who is going to be held up as a hero, although you can have more than one and they don't necessarily need to be alive. The living person can be more like a mentor on some level. You can define the role any way you want. In 12-Step programs there are sponsors, and quite often these sponsors become heroes because they are lifesavers.

You can even "connect" with and emulate a hero who is no longer living. Gandhi is dead and I'm not going to literally ever talk to him, but every time I hear something he said or read about him or think about him, every aspect of me that is trying to live the way he did is emboldened. In this sense, he is still alive within me. That is how our relationship to our heroes, living or dead, becomes self-sustaining.

I still have relationships with my parents even though they're dead. The energy inherent in a human being doesn't end with their life. It can be just as powerful for people in many ways. Bill Clinton shook John F. Kennedy's hand and went on to become president of the United States. Kennedy might have been his hero, but Clinton's relationship with Kennedy didn't end when Kennedy died on November 22, 1963. It continued in ways that inspired and motivated Clinton throughout his life.

It's vitally important to have somebody, a hero/mentor, whom you can actually sit down with in person and have a relationship with. It's equally important to identify those heroic to you, either living or dead, who you can relate to and even converse with in your head, and no, I'm not talking about acting schizophrenic. Your heroes can speak to you even if they're dead or otherwise inaccessible to you because of what you infuse the relationship with, once you have researched and understood their words, actions, and lives. Ask, for example, What would Gandhi do in this situation? How would Einstein advise me in response to this problem? How would Helen Keller have confronted this challenge? These are the kind of questions to ask yourself when you need inspiration or guidance.

It's important to emphasize that we shouldn't engage in actual hero worship. Our heroes are people with something we want, some quality or way of being. It's about emulating them. If you want to have good relationships in your life, you go to somebody who has them, who knows how to foster and nurture them, and you learn everything you can from that person.

So, while in recovery from addictions, especially when seeking a sponsor in 12-Step programs, we look for people who have some particular quality we want, or way of being, to gain information and inspiration from. Ask yourself, *Is this what I want my life to look like? Is this who I want to be? Who do I know in my life that has what I desire?* If wealth is your answer, for example, then go find that hero who has it and learn everything you can about what he or she has to offer. The more you understand how to get what you want, the closer to it you become and the better chance you have of possessing it yourself. Equally important is to not allow the pursuit or acquisition to destroy you, because it's not just the bad things that destroy us in our lives, it's also the good things improperly handled.

Will What You Fear Eventually Get You?

IF YOU have low self-worth, particularly if it is based on not finding and expressing your authentic self or your true path in life, you can actually shrink the size of your brain, resulting in memory loss and overall mental decline. OK, your first reaction to that statement might be incredulity, but there is science to back this up.

A study done at McGill University in Montreal surveyed ninety-two senior citizens over a fifteen-year period using brain scans and questionnaires. The brains of folks with low self-worth had atrophied until they were one-fifth smaller than the people who felt good about themselves. They also performed worse on memory and learning tests. Moreover, a self-fulfilling prophecy factor was found—anxiety about memory loss leads to negative thinking, which in turn can trigger the very mental impairment that was feared.[5]

cont'd. on next page

---

5 Jens C. Pruessner et al., "Effects of self-esteem on age-related changes in cognition and the regulation of the hypothalamic-pituitary-adrenal axis," *Annals of the New York Academy of Sciences* 1032 (Dec 2004): 186–90, doi:10.1196/annals.1314.017.

cont'd. from previous page

A subsequent study, in 2005, by the same team of McGill researchers found this brain atrophy phenomenon occurring in young people twenty to twenty-six years old. But the effect was also found to be reversible if self-worth is rebuilt by first focusing on gratitude for the positive things in everyday life, however tiny and seemingly insignificant those things or moments might be. This exercise helped boost self-esteem by lowering stress and raising the "internal locus of control," a person's perception of being in control of his or her outcomes in life.[6]

CREATE YOUR OWN VISION BOARD

If you can't create a vision of the life you want, you can't bring it into reality. That's from Terri Cole, licensed psychotherapist and life coach in New York City, CEO of Live Fearless and Free, and someone who has been sober since she was twenty-one years old. She wrote her master's thesis on the therapeutic properties of 12-Step programs.

She recommends you put together a visualization board. "We know how important it is to visually see things like drawings, photographs, even written word statements," said Cole. "What you focus on grows. I tell my clients to craft a vision of what they want more of and less of in their life. It can be about their health, sobriety, wealth, spiritual life, relationships. Keep those lists where

6 Jens C. Pruessner et al., "Self-esteem, locus of control, hippocampal volume, and cortisol regulation in young and old adulthood," *NeuroImage* 28 (Dec 2005): 815–26, doi: 10.1016/j.neuroimage.2005.06.014.

they can see them. Then they should visualize themselves successfully doing what is on their vision board."

Let's say that you want to travel more in the coming year. Maybe you want to visit Hawaii. Cut out or print out some pictures of Hawaiian beach and mountain scenes, along with images of a suitcase and an airplane. Place those images alongside a photo of you and whoever you are taking on the trip. Post all of this on your refrigerator or on a bulletin board, along with some appropriate sayings, such as, "We are having a wonderful time in Hawaii."

Every time you see your vision board, picture yourself excitedly packing just the right clothes for the trip. Visualize yourself getting off the plane in Hawaii and being engulfed in that warm island air. See yourself on a beach. Allow yourself to feel what it will be like. Use all of your senses.

"Your thoughts project energy waves, as do your feelings," said Cole. "Your feelings are like little hooks that snag like things and bring them back to your experience. Your thoughts and your feelings must be aligned with your goals. I call this *the harnessing of the power of your intention.*"

Obviously, if you want to be in Hawaii and you don't have enough money to pay for the trip, it can be an impediment to realizing your vision. You need to visualize what is blocking you. Why are you short of money? Maybe you need a second job and another source of income. Maybe you're spending foolishly and if you just began saving that money instead, you could cover your Hawaii expenses. Make a list of ways you can raise the money you need and post the list where you can see it every day. Visualize yourself overcoming any barriers to achieving that goal.

Simply put, said Terri Cole, you must

know it,
see it,

feel it,

and believe it . . .

to bring it.

"Many people, especially women, are embarrassed to admit what they really want in life," Cole explained.

You must be okay with what you want. Love is one area where a lot of people think they've missed the boat. Many women don't think they have value unless they are married. If you think it's too late, it is, because it becomes what you think it is. It's not too late. You're not too old. You just need to download another blueprint for what you can do with your life. That's true with addiction recovery. That's true with changing careers. You may have four or five more careers in you, if you really do an inventory of all your strengths and skills.

Often the only thing that stands in a person's way is unchecked fear. Fear is a feeling, not a fact. You can deconstruct the negative blueprints you are operating from. Mindful meditation practices are what I teach my clients to bring in present-moment aware- ness to replace projecting their fears into the future. Remember, you are the sole architect of your life experience. One of the first things my clients learn is to be willing to take responsibility for their decisions and their lives. This is a huge cornerstone for change that can help anyone visualize the life they want.

What are your unchecked fears? What are the nonsense stories you repeat to yourself, stories that ultimately obstruct your prog- ress in achieving your goals? Cole identifies a four-step process to answer those questions.

First, list all of the negative tales you cycle through your thoughts. These could be things you tell yourself you cannot do, or ways in which you put yourself down as a result of self-loathing rather than humility. Are you lying to yourself about your capabilities because you are afraid of failure?

Second, once you identify the lies you tell yourself, use a journal to trace how these false beliefs about yourself came about. Was it something that happened to you in childhood? Was it something that someone said or did to you? Connect what happened to you to your feelings about what happened. Read what you have found to someone you trust; let them witness. Next, burn the list to help put those toxic experiences into the past and out of your mind.

Third, rewrite the script of your life. Whatever you have identified that doesn't work for you, write it out of your life. You have a choice. You are the screenwriter of your life story, past, present, and future. Choose what you experience and how you think in ways that empower you.

Finally, reinforce the impact of your new life script by writing affirmations, the statements you know to be true about yourself. By using positive language in the present tense and repeating these messages out loud or silently to yourself, you begin to free your mind from all the negative-thoughts baggage you've been lugging around. If you want to bring more love from others into your life, for example, you might use this affirmation: "I am grateful and happy that I am a loving person who other people love." Then be proactive. Do random acts of kindness and love. When your inner feelings and outer expressions are in alignment, you will be a magnet attracting what you really want.

There is a saying in the recovery community that you don't think your way into right acting, you act your way into right thinking. You have to act as if you really believe in this new script for your life.

Make a List of Positive Daily Actions

TO HELP create a blueprint for daily living that supports the vision you have created for yourself, Terri Cole recommends writing down or typing up a list of positive actions to assist you in staying on track toward your goal. The idea is that when you write something down, you are more likely to actually do it.

Here is Cole's own personal daily list:

- Meditate
- Green Goodness (eat/drink my greens)
- Hydration
- Shake My Booty (exercise)
- Bells and Breathing (set an alarm on my phone for every four hours to stop and take five deep breaths)
- Pay It Forward (do at least one random act of kindness)
- Pick My Mantra (select a word or phrase to focus on today)
- Feeling State (how do I want to feel today)
- Be Courageous (take one leap of faith today)
- Gratitude (throughout the day, write down everyone/thing for which I am grateful. When you feel gratitude, you draw more experiences into your life for which to feel grateful.)

(For more information about her visualization board and taking daily positive actions, visit Terri Cole at www.terricole.com.)

GUIDE YOUR MIND TO RESHAPE YOUR LIFE

Practicing visualization or guided-imagery exercises may not only help you to imagine the type of life you want to create, but also provide you with a useful tool to help make that image of yourself a reality.

Research studies show the important impact your imagination, enhanced by visualization exercises, can have on the healing and health of your body, particularly in boosting immune system effectiveness. At the College of Medicine at the University of Arkansas for Medical Sciences, for example, researchers documented how a thirty-nine-year-old woman used imagery to change a positive test for the chicken pox virus into a negative test, and then back again, simply by imagining the virus diminishing in size and then growing. In a review of forty-six guided-imagery studies performed by the American Cancer Society, a clear pattern of evidence surfaced that the technique can be effective in reducing stress, anxiety, depression, and the pain associated with cancer treatment.

Our thoughts can quite literally reshape the strength and size of our bodies. Two studies from 2007 demonstrated that. In the first, thirty male Canadian university athletes were divided into three groups: the first did nothing beyond their daily routine; the second group did two weeks of focused strength training for one specific muscle three times a week; and the experimental group listened to CDs three times a week, CDs that guided them to imagine and visualize themselves doing the same workout as the exercise group. The result: Those who did the visualizations saw a 24 percent gain in muscle strength, comparable to the 28 percent gain achieved by those who were actually exercising. How did that happen? No one knows for certain, but the prevailing theory is that mental imagery releases hormones that accelerate muscle growth, while other brain chemicals affect metabolism to burn calories faster.[7]

The second study supports this idea and takes it even further. Harvard University researchers recruited eighty-four female room attendants at seven different Boston-area hotels and divided them into a control group and an experimental group. The controls did nothing out of their ordinary work routine and weren't given any special instructions, whereas those in the experimental group were told that cleaning hotel rooms is "good exercise and satisfies the Surgeon General's recommendations for an active lifestyle." They were given specific examples of how their work duties provided that exercise. Though actual behaviors didn't change for either group, at the end of four weeks, based on physical examinations, the experimental group "showed a decrease in weight, body fat, body mass index, and blood pressure." The control group experienced no such changes. Amazingly, it was this placebo effect—the sheer belief that something will affect you, whether for better or worse—that produced in these women physical changes based on a perceived positive image of self. This study is more of an example of "belief imagery imprinted" rather than guided visualization, but it serves to underscore how powerful such a mind process can be.[8]

If optimal physical health and healing begins in your mind and guided imagery can help get you there, couldn't such exercises also influence the arc of who you want to become as a person and shape the kind of life you want to have?

You can use your thoughts to train your mind to affect your emotional relationships with yourself and other people. And you

---

7 Erin M. Shackell and Lionel G. Standing, "Mind over matter: mental training increases physical strength," *North American Journal of Psychology* 9, no. 1 (2007): 189–200.

8 Alia J. Crum and Ellen J. Langer, "Mind-set matters: exercise and the placebo effect," *Psychological Science* 18 (Feb 2007): 165–71, doi:10.1111/j.1467-9280.2007.01867.x.

can do it in ways that bring about the changes you desire to make real the future life you envisioned.

DOING IT IN PRACTICE

It's important to set aside at least ten minutes a day to devote exclusively to perfecting your visualization technique.

First, gather up three or so small items from among your possessions—a fork, keys, ballpoint pen—anything you choose, as long as they have different colors and shapes.

While sitting upright, quietly and comfortably, set the items out side by side on a table in front of you. Separate the items by at least six inches.

Focus your gaze on the first item on the left and do so for a full minute, pretending you are taking a mental time-lapse photograph. Memorize every detail of the object.

Now close your eyes. Bring up the object's image in your mind and visualize every detail you possibly can. Keep your inward gaze fixed on this image and hold it in place for as long as you can until it begins to fade.

Next, try the second object, going through the same steps. Then the third. The next day, pick out three different objects for more visualization practice.

Your goal is to continue developing your focus day by day until you are able to keep the visualization clear in your mind, with as much realism as possible, for five continuous minutes at a time without it fading from view.

You can also practice this technique with people and scenes in your life, recalling details and feeling your emotional connection to them. Those feelings of connection will, with practice, make the technique more powerful and effective.

VISUALIZING YOUR NEW LIFE

By practicing all of the steps necessary to bring the new you from mental imagery into reality, you are not only developing a greater capacity for concentration and memory with these guided-visualization exercises, but also establishing a foundation for keeping this new vision of yourself clearly in view.

Think and Grow Rich by Napoleon Hill, and a more recent derivative called *The Secret,* teaches timeless practices designed to make manifest the kind of life you fantasize about. The key principle behind the approach was described decades ago by Hill: "Our brains become magnetized with the dominating thoughts which we hold in our minds and . . . these 'magnets' attract to us the forces, the people, the circumstances of life which harmonize with the nature of our dominating thoughts."

Thoughts are things, wrote Hill, and their manifestation into reality begins with desire, solidified by faith, which he described as the visualization of desire. Faith is a state of mind that can be induced by autosuggestion to influence the subconscious. According to Hill, these are the important first steps to programming oneself for achievement, and they are primarily based on Hill's conversations with the legendary tycoon Andrew Carnegie about how he envisioned and then lived his own remarkable life.

Guided-visualization exercises can be used as a powerful tool toward achieving your long-term goals, because the technique provides the autosuggestion programming of your subconscious mind, which Hill identified as essential to becoming the person you want to be.

Once you have become adept at using the visualization exercise with simple objects that I described earlier, it will be time to expand your practice by visualizing the kind of person you want to be and kind of life you want to live, and keeping that image fixed in your mind for at least ten minutes every day. This must become a priority and a commitment if you expect results.

You can also further strengthen the impact of these visualization exercises by reciting a mantra every day. Your mantra (a meaningful sequence of words) might be something uplifting and general, such as "I will do everything in my power to be a better person." Or it can be more specific and straightforward: "I already *am* successful and content." Whatever mantra you choose to repeat, it should support your visualization images.

The visualization process is work, not magic, and there is no guarantee of complete success. But if you are determined and persistent it will be beneficial, if only by incrementally changing how you view yourself and how you relate to others.

(For more about Lesson #3, including the results of several research studies, visit our website, www.Recover2Live.com.)

LESSON #3: PARTING SHOT

Yes, it's a time-worn (and worn out) job interview question, but ask it of yourself nonetheless: Where do you see yourself five years from now? Think it through for a minute or so. Consider not only geographic location, although that's certainly important, but also the job, career, profession, or vocation . . . What is your passion? What would you truly like to be doing with most of the hours of each day? That's the future to focus on. And with whom—if anyone—would you like to share that passionate life?

Do any of those pictures, those visualizations, make you smile? If so, take a first step today—right now—to make those images real. Change something, even if it's small, to point yourself in the direction of that goal . . . Maybe you didn't hear me: I said take a first step. Put down this book and do it *now*.

LESSON #4

REALIGN YOUR RELATIONSHIPS

And the day came when the fear of remaining tight in a bud
became more painful than the risk it took to blossom.

—ANAÏS NIN

People in recovery from addictions usually need to break
free of toxic or codependent relations with others to sustain sobriety. Imagine how much more contented we all
might feel if everyone periodically realigned or ended
their relationships that were no longer healthy, and instead
sought out more positive, trustworthy companionship.

MEET DR. STEPHEN MCCORMACK, a founder or cofounder of eight different major companies in the health care industry. He knows what surprises business can bring. Unpredictability and volatility erupt more often in our business relationships than in any other area of our existence, outside of marriage and family life. This is especially true if we are in business with a friend.

With a partner and friend, Stephen founded a $100 million company that seemed to be on the road to huge success, until the partner unexpectedly forced Stephen out by lining up the investors against him. He was out of the partnership and lost a substantial stake in the company. At about the same time, Stephen's father died. It was a double whammy and a doubly painful loss.

Under "normal" circumstances, Stephen might have felt crushed and betrayed by the vagaries of friendship and fate. But Stephen had years of recovery principles to fall back upon, which had prepared him to transcend the events that were rolling over him. Though there wasn't a silver lining to be found in his father's death, losing a business and colleague became an opportunity for Stephen to practice "the zen of surrender" and see this unforeseen "realignment" as a chance to rebound and once again prosper and grow.

"I could have been vitriolic and blasted my partner and the investors," Stephen explained to me. "But that's not who I am anymore. Recovery lessons brought me to an emotional maturation point. Surrender is so foreign to most of us, especially in the corporate world, yet it's not about giving up, it's about having hope and faith that there is something on the horizon, something better I am meant to do."

When you face one of these relationship challenges, Stephen advised that you try out what he does: "Blow off some steam, read a book, shoot some hoops, or walk along a trail. Yes, what happened perturbed me a bit, but it kind of rolled off. That sort of thing doesn't get internalized in the same manner as it used to. By stepping back, you take control of yourself, and you're not going after somebody and mentally torturing yourself."

Adopting a mindfulness nonreactive approach would do wonders for employee relations in a corporate culture. "Morale would go up, efficiencies would be heightened in the corporate structure, huge amounts of money would be saved, and there would be more continuity in business programs," Stephen noted. "Recovery lessons are not just about avoiding the use of addictive substances; it's a whole set of ideas about a way of life and living in harmony. Who wouldn't benefit from that?"

The literature of Alcoholics Anonymous tells us that the root cause of our alcoholism (or drug addiction) can be traced to our defective relations with others. That's a truism I've seen in my own life and in the lives of countless other people. These defective relationships may actually be a root contributing factor—if not the cause—of most problems afflicting the lives of addicts and non-addicts alike.

Similar to a "hero's journey" described in a Joseph Campbell myth story, journalist David Sheff's experience with his son, Nic, underscores how family dysfunctions that surface during addiction, or in the midst of any family trauma, usually result in lessons being learned the hardest possible way, which often means finally dispensing with denial and codependency to bring about radical realignments of relationships.

Nic was an honor student and school athlete when he got hooked on methamphetamine as a teenager. Nic's father, David, along with Nic's mother and two younger siblings were all sucked into the vortex of Nic's addiction drama as he spiraled into a deepening pattern of lies, thefts, betrayals, and eventual homelessness, interspersed by a series of revolving-door rehab visits.

When the home phone would ring at three in the morning, David would answer, dreading to hear what trouble Nic had gotten himself into again. As the months of addiction drama took their toll on David and his family, he felt his life falling apart from the constant worry and guilt. Eventually he suffered a brain hemorrhage and almost died, an event he attributed to being incapacitated by the perpetual stress caused by his son's addiction antics and suffering.

David began attending Al-Anon meetings for the families of addicts, and the advice he heard about the need for self-care sank in. "I realized that everything I had tried to do to help my son hadn't worked, yet I was doing the same thing over and over again expecting a different result," David told me. "My need for control grew greater as I tried to control and protect my kid, to keep him from using meth. I realized that I needed to function for my family and to care for myself and stay alive. So I had to let go of my son. This didn't mean I had to stop caring about him or loving him. I just had to let go of the fantasy that I could decide for him whether he lived or died."

Every time Nic had disappeared, David had tried to rescue him and drag him back into drug rehab. That happened at least four times. Now David had to try a different approach. When Nic phoned again asking for help, this time after a two-week disappearing act, David was firmer with him that he had ever been.

"I'm in trouble. Will you come and get me?" said Nic.

"No, I will only come and get you when you are really ready to go into treatment," replied David, who then abruptly hung up the phone.

Though letting go of his son "went against every cell in my body," David knew the codependency had to be broken and their relationship realigned. There was no other rational choice.

This new tough-love approach eventually worked. A critical juncture in the father-son relationship had been reached, which even Nic would one day recognize and acknowledge. It was Nic's last major relapse.

David wrote about these wrenching events first in a *New York Times Magazine* article, then in his well-received book, *Beautiful Boy: A Father's Journey Through His Son's Addiction.* Many of those who wrote to him after the book's publication in 2008, told David that it was his cathartic letting-go of his child that moved them to tears and resonated with them about their own experiences dealing with an addicted loved one.

"Parents have such terror and desperation to make their pain go away when a child is addicted," said David, in one of the conversations I had with him after his book was published. "But outside of addiction and recovery, there is still the same sort of huge insecurity around all kinds of relationships, whether it's marriage or business or in our social lives. Often this insecurity shows up as a need to be needed, the classic codependency. Most of us are controlled by our fears. That's where the lessons of Al-Anon can be useful for anyone. If you are in a relationship and suffer and act like a victim because of it, that is unnecessary pain you are inflicting on yourself. When we confront our fears and move through them, realigning relationships as we need to, we realize there is a lightness and joy on the other side."

WHEN THE RELATIONSHIP VOLCANO ERUPTS

Having defective relations with others complicates the life of practically every person on the planet at some time or another. We even see this phenomenon play out among entire cultures and countries due to misunderstandings, fears, and conflicts, with the resultant strife, death, and destruction.

If you haven't found your authentic self, your recovery from a toxic compulsion is going to be more tenuous. When you're a drug addict or alcoholic, no relationship in your life is authentic. Relationships are based on what you need to do to keep that whole addiction dance going.

For those struggling with addictions, their illness affects every relationship they have, usually with cyclone-like intensity. "Except for my drinking buddies, I had lost every significant relationship I had," explained Dan Duncan, who got sober at age thirty-one, more than three decades ago. "I lost my parents' trust. I lost a love relationship because of my alcoholism. People were disappointed in me. I had let them down. To stay in recovery I had to decide which relationships were healthy and which weren't. I had to let go of all the relationships that were based on alcohol. It was a complete realignment. That was the only way I could prove to myself and others that I was serious. I didn't go out and evangelize recovery or wag my finger in everyone's face, but unknowingly I set an example and a few years later, several of my drinking buddies got sober too."

Dan Duncan's experience underscores how a life not consciously connected to other human beings is a life not seriously lived. The more connections you have, the more helpful you are to other people, the more engaged you are in your community, the better your quality of life, and the more contentment you bring to yourself. In my experience, the people who are on a recovery path seem to have a connection to life that's more honest, more full, and more real, especially with their relationships to others in recovery programs.

My dad was an only child and became a movie star and an alcoholic. I saw my father once or twice a year, and he had no idea how to deal with his children. It broke his heart. He was unable to stop drinking and have good relationships, so all of his friendships went away. Some would say it was all due to alcoholism. It wasn't. Alcoholism and drug addiction just medicate. The real issue is an inability to relate to others, which is a human condition.

It goes still deeper than that. In *Recover to Live* I discussed the research work of Prof. Allan Schore at UCLA's Geffen School of Medicine. His theory, supported by research, states that if you don't bond with a caregiver by two years of age, you will either experience high levels of anxiety (hyperarousal) or feelings of being disconnected from self and surroundings (dissociation) as you get older. The result will be difficulty with regulating your emotions, a condition that in turn triggers a compulsion to self-medicate with drugs or alcohol.

When I was about fourteen years sober, I suddenly began to realize that I had this huge desire to have my own life, to figure out what I wanted, who I was, what I wanted to do, what kind of relationships I wanted to have—just about everything. This desire was volcanic and I ended up divorcing my wife. After six months of talking to a therapist about my life and how I came from a codependent family and had never individuated from that, he looked at me one day and asked, "What about your kids?"

Up until that time, I had been acting out the version of me that was basically what I learned from my family. It was the example set by my Uncle Bobby, which was, "Come on, let's go guys! We're going to go climb the mountain, go down the river." It was endless activity. I became a version of Doctor Fun—"Everybody get in the car. Come on, we're going to go someplace."—but it wasn't really me. My uncle's version was what I thought it was like to be a father. There's nothing wrong with that model. It just didn't originate with me.

During six months of talking to the therapist about leaving my wife, realigning all of my relationships, and getting my own life, I had never mentioned my kids. So when the therapist asked me, "What about your kids?", I realized I had become my father, the man who could turn away from his life and children and never look back. I went, "Oh hell, my kids."

The therapist proceeded to explain, "Listen, you can do whatever you want, but the most important thing is that you don't create unconsciously what was done to you by your parents, which is codependency. It's an unconscious relationship with other people that's dependent on a lot of things you're not even aware of."

In that conversational moment of self-revelation, I made a conscious decision that my kids were going to be a major part of my life. But my kids had a whole different idea. They were understandably pissed off and didn't want anything to do with me. I tried to encourage them to live in my house, but they didn't want to even try. I tried to get them to have dinner with me, but they didn't want to. I battled for five years. It was unpleasant. I didn't do the realignment very well, but I did it because I was conscious and sober, and I had made a choice that I wanted to have an honest, open relationship with my kids.

It's much easier to live in the family dynamic you came from and simply re-create that. But it's not very satisfying, and you tell a lot of lies living that kind of life. Having done it both ways, I can now say that my relationships with my kids today, though not perfect, are real and based on openly sharing our truths and values.

WHEN SHOULD RELATIONSHIP
REALIGNMENT OCCUR?

Relationships are often our greatest source of support and comfort. They can also be our greatest source of stress, pain, and frustration. Anytime we interact with another person or group of people, some level of relationship is happening. How we relate to others has a direct effect on our mood, stress level, physical and mental health, and, of course, our happiness. By the same token, how we relate to others is also directly affected by our mood, stress level, physical and mental health, and level of happiness.

People who have overcome drug and alcohol problems have often struggled with relationship issues from an early age, and this usually continues into recovery. As a sixty-year-old educator told me, "I really had to work on relationships when I sobered up from drugs and alcohol. In recovery I learned that the first relationship you have to get straight is your relationship with yourself. You have to repeatedly ask, Who am I really? What are my needs in relationships?"

Anytime you feel stuck in a relationship—whether romantic, friendly, or work-related—you need to examine the nature of that relationship. We try to change situations and people around us, yet, sometimes, it is not going to change. You can bang your head against the wall until it hurts, but it's still not going to change. That's why self-knowledge is so important. All relationships involve compromise, but you do not give up your own needs to keep a relationship going. If you do, you will never be "happy"; there'll always be a strain. You'll grow to resent the relationship, further aggravating the situation for everyone involved.

We each need to be an equal partner in relationships. You have your needs, I have my needs, and neither set of needs should be sacrificed. Always ask yourself, *What will work for me now?*

What's a better choice *for me*? This doesn't mean being selfish and self-centered; it simply means not losing yourself in the relationship and not letting your needs be subsumed.

Let's say you examine a relationship and it's clear it's not going to change for the better. You realize you will have to accept that this is how it is and how it is going to remain. Are you OK with that? If you are, you stay in the situation and you work with it. If, on the other hand, you decide you are not OK with the relationship and you don't believe it can change, you have to move on.

A major source of frustration, stress, and even pain in relationships is when you realize the situation isn't going to change for the better because it *cannot* change. Yet you may not be able to move on. Why? Hope springs eternal. We're social beings and we really want relationships to work out. With some people we may have a history of good times, we feel invested in the relationship, and we keep thinking (hoping) if we stick around long enough the other person will "break down" and give us what we think we need.

Write this on the palm of your hand if you need to: *No one can give you what they do not have.* Simplistic example: You come to my door needing to borrow a welding torch. I don't own a welding torch. No matter how much I want to lend you one, I don't have one to lend you and I don't know where to borrow one for you. That is not going to change.

Now think in terms of a romantic partner or friend. Many of us go through life with some degree of unaddressed self-loathing (low self-esteem). Addicts are especially afflicted with that one. We don't love ourselves well, and we're not always good at knowing or meeting our own needs. So if you know your partner well enough and you feel you are not getting what you hope for in the relationship, ask yourself this: Does this person love him- or herself well? Is she mindful and accepting of her own needs? Does he respect himself? If the answer is no, forget about getting your needs met in that relationship. It's not that the person doesn't want to change but simply that he or she can't change. You might try counseling. Otherwise, you either need to accept the situation the way it is now, or you need to move on.

People say to me all the time, "God, I wish I could leave this relationship." Or they say, "I wish I didn't have this problem with my parents or my kids." There's something not working, and they don't know what to do or where to start. They believe the biggest problem is that the other person won't change his or her behavior. They don't see their own parts in it.

People also frequently say to me, "My kid is addicted. What do I do for them?" I tell them to get support and attend a meeting of Al-Anon and they say, "What?" They think I'm crazy for suggesting they need help, too, and I reply, "If you really want to help your kid, help yourself first." The most powerful thing you can do to help a kid is to change the dynamics in the family, which you can do yourself without the kid.

You must set clear boundaries, much as David Sheff eventually did with his son. Say to your kid, "If you want to stay sober, I'll help you. If you don't, then lose my number." After doing that, go to Al-Anon and take care of yourself, because this is a family relationship illness and you also need to start getting healthy.

In his book *The Power of Now,* Eckhart Tolle made an important point about becoming "addicted" to another person: "He or she acts on you like a drug. You are on a high when the drug is available, but even the possibility or the thought that he or she might no longer be there for you can lead to jealousy, possessiveness, attempts at manipulation through emotional blackmail, blaming, and accusing—fear of loss.

"Every addiction," continued Tolle, "arises from an unconscious refusal to face and move through your own pain. Every addiction starts with pain and ends with pain. Whatever the substance you are addicted to—alcohol, food, legal or illegal drugs, or a person—you are using something or somebody to cover up your pain. That is why, after the initial euphoria has passed, there is so much unhappiness, so much pain in intimate relationships. They do not cause pain and unhappiness. They bring out the pain and unhappiness that is already in you. Every addiction does that."

It's also true that as soon as you start getting healthy and taking care of yourself and working toward your goals, your relationships start to change (realign), and not always for the better, at least in the short term. I see addicts who come out of rehab and tell their families, "I went to rehab. I'm in recovery." The families respond, "From what? We thought you just were a little angry." They refuse to believe there was a drug or alcohol problem because, if they do believe it, they may have to confront their own problems with addiction and relationships.

If you come from a culture of codependency and addiction, you're going to encounter resistance from family and friends toward the changes you're trying to make in your relationships. It's that simple. The most important thing in my life was my recovery and 12-Step groups, yet none of my family ever went to a meeting with me or ever expressed any interest. It scared the crap out of them because it forced self-examination and implied dramatic change.

If a relationship isn't working for me, I no longer act in a codependent manner for any prolonged period of time, or put up with unacceptable behavior. Nor do people get to live rent free in my mind anymore. What that means is that I no longer let other people's crap become my own. If I did, I'd be miserable. It's their stuff and I disavow any responsibility for it. I still have problems with reactivity and anger, especially when I feel misunderstood or unappreciated. But the great thing about this work is that we have a whole lifetime to make these changes.

Today, if you do something I don't like, I'll tell you about it. That creates an opportunity for me not to let stuff fester. I have healthier relationships as a result.

DO YOU MAINTAIN HEALTHY BOUNDARIES?

Addicts and people in early recovery from addictions are notorious for being unable to set and hold healthy boundaries, either in how they relate to other people or in how other people treat them. Leaky or nonexistent personal boundaries are one byproduct of having a weak sense of personal identity.

Not holding healthy boundaries in your relationships, according to New York psychotherapist Terri Cole, whether you are a recovering addict or not, is like "leaving the door to your home unlocked: anyone, including unwelcome guests, can enter at will. On the other hand, having boundaries that are too rigid can lead to isolation, like living in a locked-up castle."

Your goal should be to find a happy medium between having no boundaries and rigid boundaries, a midpoint that works best for you and advances your vision for the relationships you want to have. Like a "No Trespassing" sign erected on private property, boundaries in relationships designate the acreage of your inner and outer life that you have set aside as your own private emotional and physical space, your sacred domain.

Terri Cole describes the two types of personal boundaries as follows:

1. Physical boundaries involve your privacy and personal space, your body and the immediate space around it. An example of a boundary violation is the close talker, someone who stands too close when speaking to you. "Step back in order to rest your personal space,"

Cole advised. "By doing this, you send a non-verbal message that you feel an invasion of your personal space." Other examples include people who open your closed doors without knocking, read through your personal correspondence without permission, or touch you in unwanted or inappropriate ways.

2. Your emotional and intellectual boundaries are there to protect you from the words and actions of insensitive or aggressive people. Do you allow other people to force their preferences and points of view on you? Do you allow other people's moods to influence or determine your own mood? Do you sacrifice your own goals and desires to constantly please other people, perhaps because you fear rejection and abandonment if you don't? Social media, such as Facebook, provides one good standard by which to assess whether you are holding healthy emotional and intellectual boundaries. Do you keep people from your childhood as friends even though they constantly harangue you with their religious and political beliefs? Do you allow some of your social media friends to treat you as if you are just a consumer to be sold their products and services?

Defining and enforcing personal boundaries is dependent on your level of self-awareness and knowing who you are and what you want in life. A component of self-awareness is learning or knowing why you hold the boundaries you do, and why you fail to hold the boundaries you know you deserve and need.

Ask yourself these questions: Are you fearful that holding a boundary and saying no will result in people rejecting you? If they do reject you for having a reasonable boundary, are these really the people you want in your life? Are you someone who fears confrontation? Is that why you feel guilty when you try to hold reasonable boundaries?

BOOSTING YOUR SOCIAL WELL-BEING

Scientific studies have shown how relationships "shape our expectations, desires, and goals," observed Tom Rath and Jim Harter in their book *Wellbeing: The Five Essential Elements.* For example, a 2008 study published in the *British Medical Journal* followed more than 4,700 people over a twenty-year period and found that a person's odds of feeling happy increase by 25 percent if someone they are directly connected to in their social network is happy.[9] Both direct and indirect social network connections affect your well-being.

Other research has shown that even the happiness of a friend of your friend can affect your own feelings of well-being. It's as if subtle vibrations of happiness and well-being reach you and influence your own happiness and well-being. And those vibrations through your social networks intensify the more you are connected directly and even indirectly to happy people. This is similar to the "six degrees of separation" idea, but in the context of social networks.

"Because your entire social network affects your health, habits, and well-being, mutual friendships matter even more," wrote Rath and Harter. "These are relationships in which you and one of your close friends share a friendship with a third person. Investing in these mutual relationships will lead to even higher levels of well-being. This is why it is critical for us to do what we can to strengthen the entire network around us."

Rath and Harter examined a wealth of research data to conclude that six hours of daily social time is optimal to a person's everyday well-being. This six hours includes interactions at home,

---

9 JH Fowler and NA Chistakis. "Dynamic spread of happiness in a large social network: longitudinal analysis over 20 years in the Farmingham Heart Study." *BMJ* (Dec.4, 2008): 337;a2338.

work, on the phone, and even sending e-mails and making post-ings on Facebook, so long as the socializing occurs in a positive and supportive way. It's also important to have a best friend in your workplace because research has shown that people working alongside a close friend are seven times more likely to produce higher quality work than those who don't, and it also enhances personal well-being.

Sterling T. Shumway and Thomas G. Kimball, addictions recovery professors at Texas Tech University, wrote a 2012 book, *Six Essentials to Achieve Lasting Recovery,* that made some important points about relationships in recovery—points that apply to folks outside of the recovery realm as well. "One of the benefits or outcomes of good recovery is a greater capacity to develop and maintain good and healthy relationships," wrote Shumway and Kimball. "Relationships established through the process of recovery are more intimate, meaningful, and trustworthy."

Addiction warps relationships in numerous ways, the authors continued:

Along with boundary violations, addiction creates a culture of control, manipulation, and selfishness that strips away the uncon-ditional love/regard and likeability from the relationship . . . we say and do things that cause pain for ourselves and those around us . . . addiction is a disease of secrecy and isolation . . . it is hard to carry on a relationship with another person when you are hiding something . . . Recovery is the process of learning first how to be with ourselves, and then how to be with others . . . Recovery is a place where good boundaries are reestablished and should be respected . . . holding good boundaries is vital to the process of rebuilding trust in your relationships.

Shumway and Kimball identify four key elements essential to making and keeping boundaries in relationships:

1. Without trying to please anyone else in your life, establish boundaries that are appropriate to your needs and situation.

2. Make sure you well-define these boundaries and communicate them to other people in your life; simultaneously, you must recognize and respect other people's boundaries.

3. You must resist falling back into old patterns by protecting your boundaries against any and all attempts to breach them.

4. Over time, sometimes a long time, you may reevaluate the boundaries to make them more flexible as you feel more stable in expressing the new you. The goal in later recovery is to learn how to interact with others in more flexible ways based on the circumstances.

Visualize the Relationships You Want

"THERE IS some relational conflict somewhere in everyone's life," observed one recovery expert. "Use a diary or a journal and ask yourself, *What is the situation that bothers me, what is the context? What is my role in this and how could I react differently?*

"Rehearse the conversation you need to have with the other person beforehand. Write it down. Practice out loud or with a different person. Visualize the situation in your mind and picture a positive outcome.

cont'd. on next page

cont'd. from previous page

"When you make any change, whether in your relation-ships or in your life, you need to know what you want from the situation. Visualize what you want for yourself and how specifically would it differ from where you are now. Keep in mind that even a small change can sometimes make a huge difference, especially in how you relate to other people."

CHANGE YOUR THOUGHTS, CHANGE YOUR LIFE

"Holding onto resentment is like holding your breath," said Deepak Chopra. "You'll soon start to suffocate."

You probably know as well as I do that feeling of being stuck in life, whether in a job or relationship, which can feel like a slow but steady suffocation of your spirit. Everyone may feel this to some extent, yet these feelings take on a heightened urgency if you're also trying to shed a toxic compulsion.

Cognitive reframing (also called cognitive restructuring) is a behavioral technique that has been used with growing frequency over the past decade as a treatment for alcohol, drug, and gambling compulsions, along with eating disorders and other toxic compulsions. You may be more familiar with this process under the term Cognitive Behavioral Therapy (CBT).

CBT enables you to look differently at something or someone in your life, and do so with more honesty and self-awareness, in order to shift negative thinking into positive thoughts. We know from a mountain of research that how we think affects how we feel and act, so learning healthy ways to talk to yourself using this technique helps free you from self-sabotaging thoughts that can lead to toxic words and regrettable deeds.

Who on this planet couldn't benefit from that, especially when it comes to improving our relationships with others?

Here is how "reframing" a situation can work for you. Let's say you've been fired from your job because your company is downsizing, but you suspect it was really because you didn't get along well with your boss. You can repeatedly tell yourself (and others) a story—"I was unfairly made a scapegoat for my employer's failures and my boss had a vendetta against me"—and let that negative spin define your thoughts, emotions, and perspective on life. Or you can *reframe* the situation into a positive story you tell yourself over and over again: "This is an opportunity for me to find more compatible relationships and a more stable job that better reflects who I am and what I want to do with my life."

You don't need to lie to yourself in reframing what happened. You get to select what details to focus on. You just need to keep in mind that any story you tell is simply one point of view, and you can choose to have a more positive and healthy perspective by reframing the experience. Repeat the positive stories to yourself and others often enough and you will reshape your deeper beliefs and values.

AN EXERCISE IN HOW TO DO IT

Remember the expression "Fake it until you make it"? That practice can also work for reshaping your emotions. You can literally "fake" your way into another feeling state that helps reframe your mind-set and project a more elevated mood.

A number of different "consciousness" workshop programs use this emotion-reframing technique. Let's say you want to make yourself feel happy when you're feeling down. What are the physical and visible symptoms of happiness? Well, you smile, your energy level is up, you feel lighter on your feet, your movements are expansive, your eyes are focused, and you feel more playful.

With each of those happiness conditions in mind, try to act out each of them one at a time. Force yourself to smile. Change your posture from slouching to erect. Breathe slowly and deeply, not fast and shallow. Then get your adrenaline pumping by bouncing on your toes. Expand your range of movement. Simultaneously picture yourself in a happy place surrounded by happy people.

WHERE TO FIND IT

Many therapists now offer CBT as a healing tool to assist their clients in reframing situations and relationships.

Study evidence has also been accumulating over the past couple of years showing that self-help CBT delivered through the Internet or computer programs can improve recovery from substance abuse or depression.

Kathleen Carroll, professor of psychiatry at the Yale University School of Medicine, is at the forefront of computer-based CBT research. In a May 2012 study published in the journal *Drug and Alcohol Dependence,* she and five research colleagues used computer-assisted CBT on a group of volunteers with substance use disorders, scanning their brains with an fMRI (functional magnetic resonance imaging) before and after CBT treatment. She and her team measured distinct improvement in the decline of substance use after treatment and also saw improvement in those areas of the brain related to cognitive control, impulsivity, motivation, and attention.[10]

---

10 EE DeVito et al., "A preliminary study of the neural effects of behavioral therapy for substance use disorders." *Drug Alcohol Depend.* (May 1, 2012): 122(3): 228–35.

Numerous online CBT courses are available worldwide that are designed to help you reframe just about anything. Some are free and others require a modest fee to participate. Here are two examples:

- CBT Self-Help Programmes (www.getselfhelp.co.uk/links2.htm) provides listings for online and computerized CBT courses that you can access wherever you happen to live. The treatment courses are categorized from depression and anxiety disorders to substance abuse and eating disorders. You will also find other self-help resources for mindfulness and meditation courses.

- NPS Medicinewise of Australia (www.nps.org.au) provides CBT online resources, particularly for depression treatment, designed by psychiatrists at St. Vincent's Hospital in Sydney. Several videos on the website give more detailed information about CBT along with access to its online programs, several of which are free.

(For more about Lesson #4, including the results of several research studies, visit our website, www.Recover2Live.com.)

LESSON #4: PARTING SHOT

Most likely, there's at least one person in your life you need less of. This person pulls you down, holds you back. So do it—see less of that person. Maybe it's fewer days together per week, or fewer phone calls and texts. Start now, slowly if you must. Scale it back. Ratchet it down. Begin the fade.

Similarly, there's at least one person in your life—maybe just on the periphery—you should see a bit more of. Someone you instinctively feel will be mutually beneficial. Maybe it's a clerk at a store, a neighbor down the hall, or a cousin across town. Whatever. You know what I'm talking about. Start now, amp it up . . . slowly. An exchange of smiles. A brief conversation. Build that relationship a brick at a time.

LESSON #5

EXERCISE VIGILANCE

In many shamanic societies, if you came to a medicine person complaining of being disheartened, dispirited, or depressed, they would ask one of four questions: When did you stop dancing? When did you stop singing? When did you stop being enchanted by stories? When did you stop finding comfort in the sweet territory of silence?

—GABRIELLE ROTH

People in sustained recovery must take an inventory of their thoughts and behaviors periodically to identify self-sabotaging triggers for relapse. Imagine how much more contented everyone would feel if we all monitored and sorted out the negativity and self-deception that our minds manufacture to undermine our goals, our self-esteem, and our relations with others.

MEET LANCE ARMSTRONG. Yes, that Lance Armstrong, the amazing—but now disgraced—seven-time Tour de France cycling champion and cancer survivor. Who can forget him or the scandal he created by doping himself with banned substances before races and then not only hiding it and lying about it, but vilifying anyone who tried to tell the truth about his actions. What happened to him, including being stripped of all those championship titles, provides a cautionary tale about how much avoidable suffering is caused in the world by unrestrained attachments to power.

Vigilance is necessary to keep old patterns from resurfacing, according to the Narcotics Anonymous literature. Taking daily inventories of your thoughts and behaviors can help you stay vigilant to prevent resentments, reactivity, and old habits and behaviors from building up and sabotaging you. Though this practice was developed to help addicts sustain their recovery and prevent relapse, every human being can benefit from it.

"Lance Armstrong was as addicted to winning and power as anyone addicted to drugs," commented Dr. Gabor Maté, the Canadian expert on addiction and recovery.

> Armstrong was abused and abandoned as a child and he grew up addicted to pain and the need to be in charge, in control, and to win at any cost. He developed a lifelong rigid pattern of behavior. His true self wasn't to be a liar and a cheater. These were compensating

mechanisms he developed from childhood. He didn't really know himself. What if Armstrong had done a daily moral inventory, exercising vigilance about his thoughts, actions, and true motives? He might have seen how his addictions and attachments were controlling him. He might have saved himself and become a real champion and hero who achieved success by acting legally and morally.

For people with highly active minds, the recovery lessons in this book can help simplify their thinking and that, in turn, helps with self-monitoring. My friend, the actor John Savage, made this same point to me. If you are a movie connoisseur, you will remember John for his brilliant performances in *The Deer Hunter, Hair, The Thin Red Line,* and dozens of other films.

"During the day when my mind is racing, I've learned not to rush, not to worry," John explained. "I have to take a deep breath and then I slow down. Putting distance between feelings and reactions is something I had to learn in recovery. Like driving down the freeway and someone cuts me off. I take a deep breath and try not to react. Usually I succeed. Vigilance in the moment gives me an alternate perspective on how I should behave. It's like a new pair of glasses I look through, one breath at a time."

My exercise of vigilance frequently involves realigning my relationships. (See Lesson #4.) I believe relationships can be salvageable, but you've got to do the work and that means risking a lot. It means going into a room for a few days with somebody who knows what they're doing to excavate and deal with your core issues. If you're not willing to do it, you don't get to have a relationship with me. Lance Armstrong could have benefitted from vigilance not only about his core values and motivations, but also in applying that personal inventory to the people he surrounded himself with, and realigning those relationships until he had support from principled people who couldn't be easily intimidated.

So by taking a daily inventory, I become clear about the importance of having other people around me who are living a similar way. This whole process is challenging, it's difficult and painful, and it can be scary. If you don't have people around to tell you the truth about what you're doing and what you're not doing, you may delude yourself. The people I choose to have around me tell me the truth, not what they think I want to hear. That is part of a daily inventory. That's vigilance.

"When I did get sober, and particularly as I wrote my first inventory, my feelings began to change," wrote Kevin Griffin in his book *One Breath at a Time: Buddhism and The Twelve Steps.* "I began to see my own part in the problems I had with my parents, to feel compassion for the difficulty they had raising me. Finally seeing and accepting my own failures helped me to accept my parents' failures." This process using inventory as a maintenance tool also enabled Griffin to forgive his parents, and in so doing, he wrote, "I was freeing myself."

For Los Angeles native Monique Moss, founder of the public relations agency Integrated PR, practicing daily vigilance yielded a big payoff. Her moment of clarity came when she was doing her personal inventory while standing in front of a mirror. Taking personal inventory means mentally going through a sort of checklist of what is working and not working in your life, or even just what you are feeling in the moment.

"I realized in front of that mirror that I didn't know everything and that I had been too arrogant to ask for help," Monique told me.

I realized this had been holding me back for a decade in reaching my full career potential. There was a moment of acceptance of my arrogance. I hadn't been able to raise my hand to ask a question since I was a teenager. That realization was a game changer and led me to start a journey of postgraduate education. I now have a double master's degree in strategic communication. I took that moment of clarity and applied it to how I can be more competitive with my peers. It was vigilance in the moment that enabled me to see that I was stuck in my career because my learning process had stopped. The moment of clarity, when I acknowledged needing help, was also the start of repairing my relationships with my siblings, my teachers, and elders who have helped guide me. It has completely enriched my life.

I feel like I have reverted back to the hope, desire, and potential and vision of when I was thirteen or fourteen; the excitement of opening up my eyes and thinking, *How can I make myself a better person no matter what the situation?* The idea of vigilance for me became all about education and being open to being teachable. Vigilance helps me to be more mindful. I can't emphasize this enough. Being vigilant in taking that daily inventory is so beneficial. I know that nothing I do today will put those mental handcuffs on me again; I know that I won't be in bondage to habituated thinking again, so long as I exercise vigilance.

WRITE DOWN YOUR PERSONAL INVENTORY

We can convince ourselves of just about anything. We can talk ourselves into almost anything. A good tool for keeping your inventory is writing things down. If you write it down and study it, you can really see what is going on in your life. It's part of your reality check. If you just let it run around in your head, you can manipulate it to be whatever you want, which usually isn't going to be very healthy.

There are times when I think about unfortunate events or some of the misunderstandings I've had with people and I get mad. But the anger lasts for only about five minutes or so and then goes away. Most people live with resentments their entire life, and it eats them up and gives them diseases like cancer. If you do this kind of reflective inventory work, exercising daily vigilance, you're constantly tilling the soil of your consciousness to stay in healthy balance.

Recovery requires constant vigilance by establishing a protocol of daily behavior. The major difficulty when using vigilance is being consistent. How do you hold yourself to something that doesn't seem immediate, especially when you know it takes time? In recovery, the motto is to take in ninety meetings in ninety days—certainly a radical transformation for most people. The benefits of such a regimen don't seem readily apparent, so you need an element of trust and faith that those benefits will be realized.

Just like with food, what you put into your body either energizes or depletes you. To move toward a meaningful life of contentment, practice vigilance and find a group of like-minded people—a community—because they will reflect back to you a sense of purpose and possible solutions to the challenges you face. Community reinforces the idea that it's not just about you. That's why addicts get together in recovery groups and in 12-Step programs to work a set of steps and perform service for others. These principles are effective in practice.

Doing daily inventory has changed for me over the years. Writing everything down was critical, particularly in the beginning of this process. Then over time these lessons became a natural part of my life. I ask myself each day, *Am I being honest with others? Am I being overly reactive? Am I being true to my authentic self?* Writing down the answers is a profound experience, one that initiates change, sometimes in the most unexpected of ways.

A longtime buddy of mine called me up once and asked to stay at my house in Los Angeles. It wasn't convenient for me at the time, and I was short with him when I said no. I didn't feel good about the interaction when I hung up. As you practice vigilance over time, reacting in such a way doesn't feel good anymore. You can't just sweep the incident into your unconscious and forget it. I had to call him back and apologize for my brusque reaction, for my way of communicating with him—but not for refusing to let him stay at my house. I have to be OK with not being generous sometimes, drawing those boundaries, yet doing so without the drama of making it all the other person's fault.

It's always important to have someone else on this path with you. Sharing something or hearing something about the struggles of being human, or what it takes to transform ourselves, helps root you in this journey. This is a form of vigilance. We need to hear solutions to stay out of the problems.

I am reminded that no matter what I do on any given day, I am OK in the moment. Nothing happens by accident in God's world, whatever your definition of God. At the core of all this is developing the ability to be honest with ourselves. Progress, not perfection, needs to be the goal. Always keep in mind that it's a lifetime of incremental changes that brings about the most sustainable transformation.

"If only I had that, or did that, I would be content" is a lie we tell ourselves, a damnable lie, in my experience, to avoid the awful realization that our ship has come in, but what we thought we always wanted wasn't the answer after all. Our culture has been clever about moving the goalposts. Oh, you may have this particular car, but now you need this new one to feel or be perceived a certain way. Or that fundamental one: If I only had money to be self-sufficient, I would be content. You've either heard such statements from others or generated them in your own mind. They are a trap, a seductive but deadly trap.

Sometimes our baggage works for us; sometimes we just torture ourselves. This lesson of vigilance—and this entire book—is about trying new ways of being, of seeing what works for you.

It also means being vigilant about all of the other lessons I talk about in these pages. There's that famously memorable saying attributed to Thomas Jefferson: "Eternal vigilance is the price of liberty." It's an equally apt phrase for entire countries and corporate structures, not just for individuals. You must exercise eternal vigilance if you are going to be free of all the baggage of your past, all the stuff that keeps you from achieving your goals.

While it may be hard to get a handle on the inner landscape, it's safe to say that most people are chained to their past as surely as if they were locked in a prison cell. Some people might say, "Oh, come on, that's ridiculous." But if you're honest about it, and if you think about the times you've been at the mercy of this stuff, you know you don't have the kind of life you really want. This is why people buy so many self-help books and watch self-help programs on television: They're desperate for answers for how to escape their own self-imprisonment.

HEALTHY FROM THE TOP DOWN

Emotional sobriety is a key to effectively exercising vigilance, just as emotional maturity is essential if we are to learn from our life experiences. That holds true for individuals, addicts or not, and for entire institutional structures from the top down, whether it's the aerospace industry, technology companies, financial networks—or even the addictions-treatment industry.

Many, if not most, of the people employed in the field of addictions treatment and recovery are themselves in recovery from toxic compulsions. They are usually good at their jobs because they walk the talk. They know where addicts have been because they've been there, and they know the steps and lessons involved in mapping a path to wellness.

When Mike Neatherton became an operating partner in Northbound Treatment Services in Newport Beach, California, his goal was to make the organization healthy from the top down, which meant that owners and employees would be exercising the same daily vigilance and utilizing the same lessons of recovery, just as would any new patient admitted for treatment of substance addiction.

In recovery himself for more than two decades, Mike encourages every one of his staff members to create and follow a personal mission statement. As he explained to me: "What is your personal list of priorities? How do you use those every day? How do you stay mindful of them? Mine is my sobriety, my relationship with God, my health, my marriage, my children, my family of origin, my job, and then my financial security from my job, which allows me to provide for my family. I don't want employees at Northbound to leave it at the job, but to have something to take home every day. That helps make vigilance a lifestyle rather than just a chore. Constant vigilance, when you're practicing it, never ends."

At Northbound, Mike and his coworkers deal primarily with an eighteen-to-thirty-two-year-old population. He said:

We're working with a lot of emotional immaturity and chronological immaturity. We show them you can change your life at any age. We teach them how to identify how their life has become unmanageable. Some of these folks need help with basic life skills. Let's make sure you are up on time, make sure you are brushing your teeth. What are the acts that will make you feel better than a few hours ago. These are all forms of vigilance exercise.

Vigilance is doing those esteem things every day and identifying the treatment-plan issues that need to be addressed, and how to use that plan's steps so your life changes. We just repeat this every day and move our clients through these identifiable phases and put a clinical container around them and embrace them with the feeling that this will be okay.

I know so many people in other industries outside the treatment industry who suffer from an inability to look introspectively at themselves. Whether you are an addict or not, you have the capability to unlock your self-scrutiny and self-transformative potential. Addicts don't have a monopoly on being fear-driven. There are so many people who needlessly suffer in silence, and they take that to their job site and it prevents them from becoming effective leaders in their field. We've got to take these recovery principles and make them come alive on the job.

In my opinion, the surest escape from suffering, short of death, is through constant vigilance. I know it worked for me, and it has worked for a lot of other folks who happen to be addicts and who have lived tortured lives. They found a way out. Those principles of recovery are applicable to anybody who's living with tortured feelings, self-inflicted or otherwise.

ARE YOU IN RECOVERY
FROM FEELING MISERABLE?

Once in recovery, an addict can have an enhanced, amazing life. There are plenty of people who aren't addicts who also need that. Maybe you just want to be in recovery from being a miserable human being.

Being a part of community is a big deal, so is a daily practice regimen. Journaling, as I indicated earlier, can have huge benefits in terms of getting your issues out, seeing them clearly, and then getting relief. There are plenty of people who have a difficult time communicating this stuff, even if it's just talking to another person and being honest with them about what's really going on in your life. Don't just call people up to talk about job opportunities. Call them up and go, "I'm terrified. I've got a job interview," or "I don't know whether I should do this. What do you think?"

It takes vigilance to a different level when you begin to ask, *What are my motives? What am I doing this for? Is this something I really want to do? Is this really who I am? Is this something I'm just aimlessly chasing?*

Don't forget that often overlooked element in self-inquiry called fun. It's important not to take ourselves too seriously, and we all need to try to have fun whatever we're doing. There's got to be joy in life or the boredom that creeps in brings with it the potential for addictions. Whether we realize it or not, we are all trying to get a connection to a bearable lightness of being, a state of ecstasy instead of just sort of trudging down this dark, sometimes nasty existence road until death.

You can live in the mansion or you can live in the tenement, and you can have transcendence in your heart in either place. I've been with people from all over the map on this. Some put a gun in their mouths even though they have everything, and then there are people who own next to nothing yet feel free and happy. It's all about your qualities inside and what you're holding onto and not holding onto.

That's one of the key lessons here. You can actually orchestrate your own life by being specific about what it is you want, by figuring it out, finding out who you are or really want to be, and then giving it the spiritual energy that allows the universe to respond.

Experimentation is a big piece of recovery, trying out new methods and behaviors without becoming too attached. In the early process you're probably just figuring out how to get rid of some of what you're not. There is a trust factor you must embrace so that your journey will be fruitful.

WHY ARE RESOLUTIONS SO HARD TO KEEP?

Whether you resolve to stop drinking or abusing drugs, exercise more, lose weight, or rein in your spending habits—whatever the self-improvement goal you have set—you'll most likely experience failure. Failure and relapse often occur repeatedly, which is a difficult cycle that can, over time, deplete our self-confidence and self-esteem. Does this happen because we are weak-willed and flaky? Probably not!

There is an entire field of research called "the science of self-change" that has documented how and why we sabotage ourselves once we make resolutions to improve our lives. You might be surprised to learn that the primary reason our resolve is undermined is our optimism, a trait we humans are wired to experience and that serves us well in so many respects, except when that optimism turns out to be unrealistic.

Brain researchers call our innate tendency to overestimate chances of success by setting unrealistically high goals an "optimistic bias," and most of us tend to return repeatedly to this bias even after a pattern of failure is apparent. Remember that definition of insanity that says it is "doing the same thing over and over again but expecting a different result?" We've got a version of that going on with our commitment to the resolutions we choose to make. An example of how this optimism bias may work in practice is if you decide to get into good physical shape and begin a daily exercise program. You make a commitment to go to the gym every day without fail. A week later, a schedule conflict arises that thwarts your plan. Your failure to adhere to your commitment for even a week brings on waves of self-criticism and self-doubt about your capacity to keep commitments, even if you realize that it was an unrealistic goal to begin with. As a result, you feel less inclination to try again. A more realistic and more achievable commitment would have been to promise yourself (and others, as witnesses) that you will do your absolute best to be at the gym at least three or four times a week.

Research backs up the wisdom of this flexible but no less committed approach. In a 2005 study, 119 volunteers tried to adhere to a twelve-week course of gym-based exercise after completing questionnaires about their goals and expectations. Those participants who dropped out of the course were the ones with the most unrealistically high expectations, while those completing the course had "more modest expectations of change and came closer to achieving these expected changes."[11]

A second study of "false-hope syndrome," as its Canadian researchers called it, examined how unrealistic expectations are responsible for cycles of repeated failure. Volunteers were randomly assigned to a physical-activity group, a stress-reduction meditation group, or a no-change control group. The results, matching expectations with performance, showed that both exercisers and meditators were "unsuccessful relative to their expectations," with the exercise group having "more positive expectations about their resolutions immediately after committing to them." Those who were most optimistic were the least successful.[12] Why does this happen? One particular brain chemical, released in excess, directly helps inflate unrealistic expectations. "When predicting financial profits, relationship outcomes, longevity, or professional success," concluded British researchers in a 2012 study, "people habitually underestimate the likelihood of future negative events." Their study found the key to this optimism bias is the

---

11 Fiona Jones et al., "Adherence to an exercise prescription scheme: the role of expectations, self-efficacy, stage of change and psychological well-being," *British Journal of Health Psychology* 10 (Sep 2005): 359–78, doi: 10.1348/135910704X24798.

12 Kathryn Trottier et al., "Effects of resolving to change one's own behavior: expectations vs. experience," *Behavior Therapy* 40 (June 2009): 164–70, doi: 10.1016/j.beth.2008.05.004.

release of dopamine into the brain. To demonstrate this phenomenon, the University College London research team administered a drug to volunteers that enhances dopamine production and, using a battery of tests, measured a clear increase in the volunteers' optimism bias. These findings provide strong evidence that "dopamine impacts belief formation by reducing negative expectations regarding the future." [13]

We see this dopamine link to overly rosy expectations in pathological gamblers who convince themselves the next big win is just one more bet away. As I noted in my book *Recover to Live,* one of the best antidotes is substituting a healthier form of dopamine release when the urge to gamble surfaces, activities such as rock climbing, roller coaster riding, or similar forms of excitement. This concept of substitution could be useful to anyone in any endeavor.

So, are we prisoners of our own brain chemistry and its sabotaging effects when we set and try to keep resolutions and achieve goals? Not when we become more aware about it all. The trick is to adopt techniques that prevent you from repeatedly holding unrealistically high expectations, which result in failures that erode your motivation.

Exercising vigilance has an important role to play in making realistic plans and then in monitoring them. Irrespective of the plan or goal you set, you need to have a plan for what to do when obstacles arise—and you know they always arise. If you are dieting, for example, and you have vowed to resist eating sweets, keep something healthier around that you can reflexively reach for, such as an apple, instead of just trying to resist the temptation itself.

---

13 Tali Sharot et al., "How Dopamine Enhances an Optimism Bias in Humans," *Current Biology* 22 (July 2012): 1477–81, doi: 10.1016/j.cub.2012.05.053.

Experiments have also shown that relying on the word *don't*— telling yourself "don't do this" and "don't do that"— doesn't work very well. Training yourself to ignore obstacles and distractions by having a fallback action you can quickly implement is much more effective.

TRY JOURNALING *AND* STORYTELLING

Stories and storytelling are crucial to recovery because they help penetrate the layers of denial (self-deception) that hide our awareness of the true self. As Ernest Kurtz and Katherine Ketcham pointed out in their book, *The Spirituality of Imperfection: Storytelling and the Search for Meaning,* "In bringing us face to face with our own imperfection, stories confront us with our self in a way that helps us to accept the ambiguity and mixed-up-ed-ness of our human being. Storytelling helps us to create a 'whole,' a whole that does not deny that it is made up of incongruous, fractured pieces, but whole nonetheless . . . storytelling in and of itself conveys that there are no quick fixes. The storytelling format of 'what we used to be like, what happened, and what we are like now' emphasizes a process through time and so points to the healing of time."

In his book *Willpower: Rediscovering the Greatest Human Strength,* psychologist Roy Baumeister elaborated further: "The act of telling a story forces you to organize your thoughts, monitor your behavior, and discuss goals for the future. A personal goal can seem more real once you speak it out loud, particularly if you know the audience will be monitoring you." He notes how studies of people undergoing cognitive therapy have found that their resolutions were more likely to be kept if they made them in the presence of other people. This act of witnessing and being witnessed helps to reinforce self-monitoring and willpower.

Alcoholics Anonymous, from its early days onward, has effectively used that storytelling and witnessing approach to assist people in creating a fresh direction for their lives. In a 2008 study of AA conducted at the University of Sydney in Australia, researchers Dr. Anthony Grant and Genevieve Baijan described the importance of storytelling at 12-Step meetings this way: "Members are encouraged to share their life stories with other attendees, engaging in cross-dialogue and self-parody; humorous, self-deprecating autobiographies assist members to deconstruct their alcoholic identity, relieve guilt, and reinforce gratitude and humility. Further, sharing stories facilitates the creation of a sense of community and reconnection, with participation in cross-dialogue resulting in group validation and an increased commitment to abstinence goals . . . Lastly, the process of recounting a personal history allows the member to habituate to the emotive content of their story, engaging in a form of *cognitive de-fusion* that reminds the individual of the distinction between their *emotions/thoughts/actions* and their *true selves.*"

Kurtz and Ketcham call the storytelling process "learning to follow a new map, a new way of life . . . learned and taught only through the process of telling stories—stories that disclose in a general way what we used to be like, what happened, and what we are like now . . . Through the practice of hearing and telling stories, we discover and slowly learn to use a new 'map,' a map that is more 'right' because it is more useful for our purposes."

Writing with brutal honesty in a journal where you reflect, tell the stories of your life, and describe the challenges you have faced and overcome, or even by writing heartfelt letters you never send to anyone but yourself, are techniques that research studies show have positive effects for both your body and mind. By releasing what you have held on to for so long, you help trigger the release of tension, stress, guilt, shame, and other emotional toxins that may be holding you back or undermining you.

Written emotional expression (a therapist's term for journaling) was one of the seven self-help tools for recovery from addictions that I described in my book *Recover to Live*. The research evidence is overwhelming that the practice of journaling is beneficial to health and healing in a wide variety of ways, from lowering blood pressure to strengthening the immune system. It's also being utilized to treat addictions and assist in maintaining recovery.

Journaling and storytelling can be useful in exercising the vigilance you need to break bad habits or to reinforce your resolve to become the person you desire to be. You can even use these techniques to create imagined dialogues between yourself and other people with whom you have quarrels or unresolved issues, as a way to bolster your confidence and order your thoughts before it's time to have the actual conversations.

The late psychologist Ira Progoff, a pioneer in the use of journal therapy, studied under Carl Jung and created The Progoff Intensive Journal Program. Progoff taught that by engaging in the practice of recording your daily feelings, intuitions, dreams, and perceptions of life events, you come to better realize and understand your inner strengths and see expanded options in life. Just as important, journaling can give life deeper meaning by developing a heightened spiritual awareness.

(For more about Lesson #5, including the results of several research studies, visit our website, www.Recover2Live.com.)

LESSON #5: PARTING SHOT

Do this for one week and see what you think: At the beginning of each day, make a to-do list. Yes, I know, but just hear me out. Make a list of six, eight, twelve, whatever specific items for that day. Create the list on your smart phone, tablet, or—God forbid—on a piece of paper. Include appointments and meetings, of course, and work tasks and family responsibilities. But also include reading for a set amount of time each day—a book, magazine, or the newspaper—and exercise time for those thirty push-ups or that treadmill walk. And schedule time for just sitting and breathing, for unshackling your mind. Schedule specific times or approximate durations for all of this. Check items off as you get them done. Do the list every day for a week and then decide if you want to do it for another week. I have a hunch you will.

CULTIVATE NATURAL, HEALTHY HIGHS

Music is a safe kind of high.

—JIMI HENDRIX

Stress can trigger relapse, so people in recovery often search for natural, healthy highs to replace addictive substances and behaviors. Imagine if we all relied on natural highs to combat stress instead of self-medicating with substances potentially injurious to physical and mental health.

MEET BLU ROBINSON. There were just six, including Blu, when the experiment began in 2011—four adult men, a young woman, and their leader, Blu—trying out group exercise as a way to keep themselves in recovery from drugs and alcohol.

Blu was already a marathoner and a licensed substance abuse counselor who had experienced firsthand how intense exercise can reduce depression and substance cravings, and as a side benefit, improve relationships. He decided to test whether the same transformation could be generated in a group dynamic.

Their first competitive run was a five-kilometer race in Provo, Utah, which might not seem like a long distance unless you take into account that no one other than Blu was anywhere near athletic. One guy had been smoking cigarettes for a quarter of a century. All of them had abused alcohol or drugs for many years.

Someone had the idea of printing up T-shirts for the group to wear during the race that read "Racing for Recovery" on one side and the slogan "Addict to Athlete" on the other.

"You know people will see that you have an addiction if you wear these," Blu warned the group. "Are you sure you want to do this?" After all, they would be running through the streets of Provo in front of hundreds of non-addict spectators, most of them Mormons, and who could predict what the reaction would be.

Everyone wanted to wear the shirts. They told themselves and each other, "We have nothing to be afraid of, nothing to be ashamed of. Let's do it!" Blu instantly grasped their meaning—they would be telling their story in public and, as he knew, great power can come from sharing your story.

They ran that race, everyone completed it, and the crowd cheered its approval. When the race was over, this small group was ecstatic with relief and joy. They huddled together at the finish line, tears streaming down their faces.

The next month another twelve people who were in recovery from addictions signed up and the Addict to Athlete idea began to take off. They launched a Facebook page and posted a video on YouTube featuring highlights from the five races they participated in during 2011. They got a basketball team together and joined the city league, wearing Addict to Athlete jerseys. They were now talking excitedly about goal attainment, not about using unhealthy substances.

"It's become a big family," Blu Robinson explained. "It's okay to do it alone, but exercising as part of a community is real-time accolades. The bonding creates strength in purpose and empowerment from numbers. We have almost three hundred athletes right now. The stigma is diminishing, and we are changing the public's perception of addiction as a weakness. I've had probation officers extend curfews for parolees because they're participating in something meaningful with us. People are seeing us now for the first time as strong human beings. With these T-shirts, the public sees walking billboards for recovery."

The idea for Addict to Athlete sprang from Blu's work at a county substance abuse center in Provo, where he first saw triathlon training being used as part of a treatment regimen. He then began running marathons himself because he found them to be spiritually uplifting. His depression faded and his relationships improved because he felt better about himself. He worked out with guys who would tell him more during one workout than they would ever reveal in a therapist's group session.

If any of the athletes want to use an addictive substance again, Blu says, "Let me take you out on a run first." Usually these prospective relapsers come back and feel so good they don't need to use. They'd rather sit in a hot tub instead of using drugs or alcohol.

If any of the athletes playing on Blu's basketball team relapse, he doesn't hesitate to bench them. In a time-out session during one recent game, a player admitted to Blu that he had relapsed, so Blu immediately took him out of the game. He was a good player and the team needed him, but he had to sit on the bench and watch his teammates struggle on the court. Afterward, he felt like he had let his teammates down. Now, whenever the guy has a craving, he goes running or dribbles a basketball.

"I tell people to slow down and look at the abundance," said Blu. "You have food in your fridge, you have shoes on your feet. That helps with accountability. We all have a choice to live in the captivity of addiction, bad relationships, a job we don't like, versus choosing a life of liberty and freedom. Everyone has someone in their family with an addiction, whether they know it or not. See him not as weak, but as someone who has been wounded. These are the people who feel too much, their hearts are so big they try to cover it up because they've been abandoned or abused. We teach them balance and service, not just physical activity. They also volunteer in races by manning aid stations where athletes get water and medical care. We create substitutes for addiction."

Research has shown that running boosts serotonin levels in the brain, triggering the release of endorphins and other brain chemicals that promote positive feelings of well-being. Running outside on trails, among the trees, releases negative ions that stimulate oxygen flow to the brain. For many people, this combination can elevate their mood as effectively as if they had taken a Zoloft or Prozac antidepressant.

The multiple benefits of exercise in general and running in particular have been highlighted in several well-received books, including 2012's *Running Ransom Road: Confronting the Past One Marathon at a Time* by Caleb Daniloff, in which he describes how, from the age of fourteen to twenty-nine, he was an alcoholic . . . "drunkenness was my calling." On the day of his high school graduation, when his famous father, journalist Nicholas Daniloff, was giving the keynote address to the student body, Caleb had been expelled from the school for his drinking and drugging antics.

Caleb took up running as a sobriety tool and participated in marathons from Boston to New York to Moscow as part of his recovery strategy. "When I took up running, I found not only a new central pattern to my life, but a forum in which to confront myself.

"I don't know whether I'll ever fully calm the waters of my past," he confessed, "but the steady drumbeat of my feet on the ground and my arms waving through the air helps. For an hour at a time, I am enduring, rebuilding."

Running, wrote Caleb, helped him to "satisfy my urge to flee without actually running away, to exorcise my cowardice, to begin slowly drilling inward . . . Every time I run, I'm having a conversation with my purest self, my moral inventory on full display. Even within the simple act of running, a seemingly monotonous activity, there can be complex, radical change."

Another book, 2011's *The Long Run,* written by recovering alcoholic and drug abuser Mishka Shubaly, offers another explanation of how running helps maintain sobriety. The focus is on how the high of exercise helps to reduce cravings. Shubaly told CNN: "For me, exercise is the opposite of alcohol. Alcohol is the easiest, fastest, and most effective way of saying, 'I don't care.' Exercise, especially for someone who has been a sedentary alcoholic for a long time, is brutally difficult. And, as such, it's a very meaningful way of saying, 'Okay, I actually do care now.'"

MOVE A MUSCLE, CHANGE A MOOD

It's been said that addicts and alcoholics are more sensitive. They feel the weight of the world more. I don't know whether that's true or not because I've never been a normal person. But I will tell you this: I've been in recovery for nearly three decades and I definitely need experiences in my life that get me out of the routines of life. Natural highs do that.

Working out at a gym can have that effect. I've exercised compulsively. Constant activity now comes naturally to me. If you're revving at high rpm's all the time, you need a way to kind of take the edge off.

"I feel the correlation between moving a muscle and changing a mood," observed Robin Shamburg, a New York screenwriter, author, and journalist. "Once I joined a gym I discovered I really liked working out. There is an effort and a reward, which for me is the endorphin rush, the exercise high." Robin's other natural highs are what many people might take for granted: her dog, whose companionship elevates her mood, and her cooking. Even when she cooks only for herself, it is the process of making something good and important that enables Robin to feel more carefree and yet, empowered.

"Everybody loves to get high. It's human nature," said Tommy Rosen, a yoga teacher and addiction recovery expert who gives yoga workshops all over the world. "The problem is that most people are self-destructive about it. If you get high on a substance or behavior that, afterward, you pay a price for, that isn't a sustainable or healthy high. We need to think of the concept of getting high differently."

Tommy has researched this idea of natural highs and has a book on the subject coming out in 2014, *Recovery 2.0: Overcoming Addiction in the 21st Century*. He has been teaching yoga for more than a decade and knows from both observation and firsthand experience that "anything you can do like yoga that detoxifies and strengthens the body, quiets the mind, and gets energy and oxygen moving will be a good thing for your mental and physical health. It's one of the best natural highs imaginable."

I've done a lot of yoga, particularly Bikram (hot) yoga. Working out in a gym gives a certain natural high, whereas yoga gives you that plus something more. Just the act of actually breathing as deeply as we do in yoga is profoundly new for most human beings. Most addicts never take a deep breath.

My yoga practice helps me breathe, which is really good in terms of keeping me present. Most addicts and alcoholics are living in their heads. Yoga forces you more or less to be in the present because of the whole commitment to breath and holding postures. There's usually some meditation attached to the practice, so there are spiritual benefits, as well as the physical and mental.

I got into yoga because I had a bad back. I was working on the television show *All My Children*, and my back used to go out all the time. In my family we grew up saying, "We Kennedys all have bad backs." So it was a kind of badge of honor in our family to have a bad back. Since I wanted to be more like a Kennedy, having a bad back was a good thing, even though it left me so paralyzed or crippled at times that I couldn't dress myself for work. So I began to practice yoga, and it changed my life. It's taken fifteen years, but I don't have those back issues anymore.

My obsession with yoga might prompt some people to ask, "Why do you spend an hour and a half or two hours a day being uncomfortable by doing this?" The answer is simple: I like it. I'm going to keep doing it because it makes me feel good. If you feel good working with children in East Africa or designing a new rocket ship or with whatever your focus is on, and it's not causing you or society a lot of harm, then do it, even if you're addicted to it.

My cousin John Kennedy Jr. went to a yoga class once, before he died in a plane crash, and after class remarked to someone, "God, I wish my father had been able to do that."

"You mean take a yoga class?" the other person replied.

"No," said John, "take a breath."

What he meant by that is that oftentimes people who are enormously successful just never take a long, deep breath. The act of breathing slowly and deeply actually produces a feeling and mental state that most people are simply unfamiliar with and would be surprised by how beneficial it can be.

My fiancée, Mercedes Miller, has always enjoyed high-energy sports like soccer and kickboxing for the endorphin release she gets. When she discovered yoga, a whole new level of natural high energy opened up for her, and she was inspired to get certified to teach yoga. Mercedes described her yoga-high transformation this way:

When I decided that alcohol and drugs weren't going to serve me, I turned my focus to yoga. No one wants to be hung over in yoga. That led me to a healthy diet and good nutrition. So yoga became an entire lifestyle, giving me clarity into what kind of energy I wanted in my life and how to obtain it.

Five years ago I had depression and I was quick-tempered. I didn't have patience and was always looking for the next exciting thing. I felt like I needed to be constantly stimulated. As a result, I was always in a state of anxiety and depression, which led to a lot of negative thinking. My yoga practice put me much more in the moment; it calmed down my energy and my restless spirit. I became a more positive thinker and I go inward a lot more with self-reflection. Other people, my friends and family, see the differences in me between then and now. Yoga has given me the free attention to be open to experiencing other parts of life and new ideas.

LAUGHTER YOGA IS SPIRITUAL MEDICINE

Humor and laughter produce some of the most natural and potent highs that we human beings are capable of experiencing. Who hasn't felt joy, elation, and mood elevation in the wake of a fit of belly-shaking laughter? It even has documented health benefits.

Magazine editor Norman Cousins first wrote about using humor to boost the natural healing capability of the body in his 1981 book *Anatomy of an Illness,* which was a landmark examination of self-healing that helped jump-start an entire new field of science known today as mind-body medicine. While battling a life-threatening disease, Cousins watched funny movies every day and consciously harnessed humor and laughter into a healing tool that helped put his disease into remission.

Dr. Madan Kataria, a physician in India, took this approach and applied it to group dynamics during the mid-1990s by creating a laughter therapy called Hasya yoga (*hasya* means laughter in Sanskrit). The idea is to learn how to laugh at ourselves with conscious, sustained regularity and, in doing so, achieve a more positive outlook on life, along with additional benefits to overall health. Laughter yoga spread contagiously from just one club, with five people practicing in a park in 1995, to more than eight thousand clubs in sixty-five countries by 2011, which indicates this is more than just a passing fad and that "unconditional" laughter can be a powerful tool for stimulating natural highs.

Each session of laughter yoga starts with a series of warm-ups—stretching the body, clapping hands, and some chanting ("ho ho, ha ha") to create a rhythmic abdominal muscle movement. This helps relax participants and lowers their shyness and inhibition levels. Next come breathing exercises to expand the lungs and prepare them for rapid intakes of air. Finally comes a "cocktail" of simulated laughter poses—making funny faces, open-mouthed silent laughter, swinging the arms in exaggerated movements—anything to trigger the laugh response. At a certain point these simulations morph into genuine, hearty, unconditional, and contagious bouts of laughing. It's a group version of "fake it until you make it." These twenty-minute laughing sessions are often followed by a short, guided relaxation exercise.

Though the medical research on laughter yoga is still in its infancy, results produced thus far show considerable promise for laughter as a therapy for many ailments, both physical (cardio-vascular health in particular) and psychological (mood elevation). Here are just two research findings:

- A 2011 study in the *International Journal of Geriatric Psychiatry* took seventy depressed elderly women and divided them into laughter, exercise, and control groups. Both the laughter and exercise groups saw their depression levels decrease, but the greatest improvement in overall life satisfaction came from those who did the laughter exercises.[14]

- In 2012, researchers at the University of Arizona Department of Surgery and Medicine utilized daily laughter yoga with patients ranging in age from fifty-one to sixty-nine, who were awaiting heart or lung transplants and suffering from psychological distress. Clear evidence emerged that the humor exercises improved heart rate variability, which is often a risk factor for transplant patients, and elevated their moods so they could better cope with the medical procedure.[15]

---

14 Mahvash Shahidi et al., "Laughter yoga versus group exercise program in elderly depressed women: a randomized controlled trial," *International Journal of Geriatric Psychiatry* 27 (March 2011): 322–7, doi: 10.1002/gps.2545.

15 Ann Baldwin et al., "Effect of laughter yoga on mood and heart rate variability in patients awaiting organ transplantation: a pilot study," *Alternative Therapies in Health and Medicine* 18 (Sep 2012): 61–6.

What harm would there be if we used laughter yoga to add levity to a wide range of group situations? How about 12-Step meetings? People in recovery need all of the humor they can summon to go with those inspiring but sometimes dark and heavy stories heard regularly in meetings.

How about in the US Congress? Imagine if every session began with lawmakers not taking themselves so seriously for a few minutes. Think of the effect that might have on their level of cooperation. The same holds true for the United Nations. Anyway, you see the implications—limited only by our imaginations.

EXPERIMENT TO FIND YOUR NATURAL HIGHS

I frequently take a very hot bath and then jump into a really cold shower. Just the act of doing this, going from one temperature extreme to another, quiets my mind and relaxes me for a period of time.

Brenda Schell, program director at the Missouri Recovery Network, made the point that anything natural that stimulates our brain endorphins is a natural high. "Helping other people makes a lot of people feel good," she said. "Doing community service can provide elevated feelings, whether it's working in a soup kitchen for the homeless or picking up trash along roadsides. The recovery community has those natural highs down. Everyone in our country needs to be taught how to get healthy highs without alcohol and drugs. That's another lesson for society from the recovery community."

Besides competitive or extreme sports, seeking an adrenaline rush in recovery often involves speed—the natural kind—on a motorcycle or in a race car. These days you see entire motorcycle clubs comprised of people in recovery. To outsiders these folks may resemble Hell's Angels, but make no mistake, they're getting their "fix" from speed on the open road rather than from drugs and alcohol.

"The same power that fuels our destructive impulses can fuel our excitement, creativity, and ambition," reads a Narcotics Anonymous (NA) publication, *Living Clean: The Journey Continues.* "We have the freedom to try new things and take new risks."

Here is how a member of NA, in a story that could be a metaphor for recovery, described his weekends climbing glaciers: "In those moments when I really am on the edge of life and death, when I'm not sure how I'm going to find my next foothold, then I feel present to the moment. I'm not thinking about the bills or the wife or the job, just how good it is to be alive and how I'm going to stay that way."

You don't need to become a mountain climber, skydiver, bungee jumper, or any other type of risk-taker or thrill-seeker to find the right natural high for you. But I do encourage you to expand your comfort zone, if only incrementally, to see what works to keep you stimulated and inspired about life and fully living it.

Music Is a Natural High

THAT'S JUST common sense, right? All of us know from firsthand experience that our preferred music can elevate our mood and enable us to transcend our worries, if only temporarily. The positive effects go well beyond the obvious soothing of feelings. It turns out the best way to get those benefits is by allowing the music to quite literally *move* you rather than to passively listen.

Endorphins are released in the human brain when it is exposed to pleasing music, but not if you're just sitting while listening. You need to actively perform or physically move to

cont'd. on next page

cont'd. from previous page

the music in order to get the endorphin "high" that is characteristic of these natural brain opiates.

In a series of four experiments conducted in 2012, British
researchers tested the effects of singing, dancing, and drumming on the brain, and all were found to trigger the release
of endorphins. In one experiment, musicians played together
for thirty minutes and compared their endorphin release—as
measured by pain thresholds—to a group of employees (sales-
people) in a music store who listened to uplifting music, also
for a half hour. The musicians who played together showed
much higher pain thresholds and positive emotions than the
store employees.

The same results turned up when a religious group, which
had engaged in singing, clapping, and upper body movement,
was compared to people at a prayer meeting where no music
was played. "We conclude that it is the active performance
of music that generates the endorphin high, not the music
itself," the research team noted. "These effects may play a
particularly important role in bonding large social groups in
humans."[16]

A NATURAL METHOD FOR MOOD ELEVATION

Every one of us does it twenty thousand times or more a day and
yet we are largely unaware we're doing it. We are even less aware

---

16 Robin I. M. Dunbar et al., "Performance of music elevates pain threshold and
positive affect: implications for the evolutionary function of music," *Evolutionary
Psychology* 10, no. 4 (2012): 688–702.

of how important doing it correctly is to our physical and mental health. As a natural physical function, breathing is taken for granted even more so than eating, yet our breath and the oxygen it provides us are just as vital to providing energy to the body and mind as the food we eat.

"If I had to limit my advice on healthier living to just one tip, it would be to learn to breathe correctly," remarked Dr. Andrew Weil, a pioneer in the field of alternative medicine, in one of his many interviews on the subject. His statement is backed up by a wealth of medical evidence that shows changing the way we breathe to absorb more oxygen can assist in relieving maladies ranging from chronic pain to depression and stress-related problems. It's well-known that stress and depression shadow just about everyone in recovery from addictions, just as these toxic shadows are an equal-opportunity affliction for "normies," as well. So using natural techniques to disperse these mind and mood shadows can have universal benefits.

Shallow breathing isn't natural. Infants are born taking deep breaths, but as we age our breaths usually become shallower, especially as life stresses take their toll. Some researchers have noted that adults usually take fifteen to twenty breaths a minute, breathing more than three times faster than what is considered necessary or healthy.

There is a domino effect to your health that can occur from shallow breathing over the course of a lifetime. When your breathing is rapid and shallow, your adrenal glands pump out cortisol and other stress hormones in response, an elevation in stress hormones that can weaken the immune system and keep your brain in a state of overarousal. This is when impacts to health begin to multiply.

In 2005, a team of scientists published the results of their study of rhythmic breathing in the *Annals of the New York Academy of Sciences,* which concluded that the ancient Indian rhythmic breathing processes of Sudarshan Kriya and Pranayam not only reduced stress in test subjects but also increased their levels of the natural killer cells that fight cancer. After six months practicing the exercises, nearly one-quarter of volunteer test subjects were also able to bring their tobacco habits under control.[17]

To counteract respiration deficiency, adopting one of the afore-mentioned ancient breathing practices (or Kundalini yoga as prac-ticed by Tommy Rosen) can be most beneficial, but you can also work any one of the following four breathing techniques into your daily routine:

1. **Slow, deep breathing:** This is a simple exercise you can do while driving a vehicle or sitting at your desk. Be aware of your breath. Take very slow, deep breaths into your belly, hold for a few sec-onds, then slowly expel the air. Practice doing this until it comes naturally to you whenever you are by yourself. This is a great easy way to release tension, especially when sitting in traffic, waiting on phone calls, or enduring business meetings.

2. **Diaphragmatic breathing:** This is good for stress and anxiety. You need to lie on your back with knees bent for this one. With one hand just below your rib cage and the other hand on your upper chest, breathe slowly through your nose pushing your stomach against the lower hand. Exhale slowly through your pursed lips while tightening your abdominal muscles and allowing them to fall inward. Keep the hand on your chest still. Try doing this exer-cise several times a day for up to ten minutes at a time.

---

17 Vinod Kochupillai et al., "Effect of rhythmic breathing (Sudarshan Kriya and Pranayam) on immune functions and tobacco addiction," *Annals of the New York Academy of Sciences* 1056 (Nov 2005): 242–52, doi: 10.1196/annals. 1352.039.

3. **Bellows breathing:** This will boost your energy and increase alertness. You can sit up for this one. Keep your mouth closed and quickly inhale and exhale through your nose. Try to achieve three of the in-out breath cycles per second. Do it for five seconds at a time, with five or so seconds of rest between each cycle, for a full minute.

4. **Alternate nostril breathing:** This ancient yogic technique for relaxation also reduces your blood pressure and boosts mental energy. While sitting comfortably in a chair, press your right thumb against your right nostril, closing it. Slowly inhale a deep breath through your left nostril. Hold the breath. Close your left nostril using your ring and small fingers, release your thumb from your right nostril, and slowly exhale through the right nostril. Do the same ritual by switching nostrils. Do this round of breathing until you start to feel more relaxed.

DO IT WHILE UNDER A HOT SHOWER

As I mentioned earlier, when it comes to natural healthy highs, one of my favorites is jumping from a hot tub into a pool of cold water and back into the hot tub again; one of the most relaxing and rejuvenating activities I have ever discovered. Scandinavians have known the benefits of this hot/cold immersion ritual for generations.

Another variation is to stand for extended periods under a hot shower. If you've ever done this and had an inspired idea as the hot water cascaded off your skin, you have demonstrated in practice a body of scientific research that has shown the energizing effects of hot showers do promote fresh ideas and insightful thinking. Try doing it while playing your favorite, most inspiring music.

A study published in *Nature Medicine* reported how stimulation of the skin (the cells of the epidermis, to be exact) during a hot shower releases beta-endorphins. "Just the stimulation itself raises the awareness level of the brain," commented Prof. Frank Rice of the Center for Neuropharmacology and Neuroscience at Albany Medical College and study coauthor. "That triggers activity that can lead to a new thought."[18]

I recommend you do some experimenting. When you need to relax or do some creative brainstorming, or if you get a toxic compulsion craving, take a hot shower for as long as you and your water heater can stand it. While you're doing that, practice the breathing exercises I described. You will double the impact *and* the pleasure for your mind and body.

(For more about Lesson #6, including the results of several research studies, visit our website, www.Recover2Live.com.)

LESSON #6: PARTING SHOT

Choose one evening this weekend to make yourself laugh, in the privacy of your home, with a friend or by yourself. Using Netflix or pay-for-view, watch a favorite comedy movie or a video of your favorite comedian, like I do. Maybe it's a classic such as *Airplane!* or *Blazing Saddles,* or something more recent such as *Bridesmaids* or one of the *Hangover* films. It can be one you've seen or one you've been meaning to see. Get some munchies, get comfortable in your favorite chair, and then push play. Now laugh and experience a natural high.

---

18 Alla Khodorova et al., "Endothelin-B receptor activation triggers an endogenous analgesic cascade at sites of peripheral injury," *Nature Medicine* 9 (Aug 2003): 1055–61, doi:10.1038/nm885.

TRANSFORM PAIN INTO GROWTH

Hardships often prepare ordinary people for an extraordinary destiny.

—C. S. LEWIS

An important technique used in recovery involves the practice of learning—and being grateful for—those unrealized gifts and life skills arising from pain, suffering, and hardship. Imagine how much more planetary contentment there would be if more people could transform painful incidents into opportunities for understanding and self-growth.

MEET TOM MCLELLAN, a man who knows personal pain. When the dreaded call came for Tom on May 17, 2008, he was vacationing at an East Coast beach house with his wife. On the phone was Tom's sister-in-law. "Your son is dead," she sobbed.

Tom's youngest son had just graduated from the University of Pennsylvania and had been partying in celebration the night before. He overdosed on a combination of alcohol and drugs and died in the sister-in-law's basement. He was the kid who never seemed to have a problem, certainly not a drug problem.

This might sound strange or even cruel, though I don't mean it to be, but Tom's life would never be the same after this tragedy and yet, the entire nation would end up being better off because of it.

No one living today had studied substance abuse and addiction more intensely and with more scholarly dedication than Dr. Tom McLellan. I think everyone involved with the substance treatment field would agree with that statement. He had been in the field for thirty years investigating new treatments, conducting research, writing scientific journal articles and grant proposals, and serving as a psychologist and professor of psychiatry at the University of Pennsylvania. He had been editor-in-chief of the *Journal of Substance Abuse Treatment,* and in 2003 he received the Life Achievement Award from the American Society of Addiction Medicine. Tom was and remains a giant in the field of substance addiction.

The sad irony is that addiction and substance abuse ran amok in Tom's family. Both his brother and father had died from it. His older son had been admitted to the Betty Ford Center just weeks before the death of his younger son. Tom debated whether he should tell his older boy that his brother had overdosed and died, fearing the timing of this news might harm the living son's recovery. Ultimately, Tom decided he must do so in person and boarded a flight to Palm Springs, where the Ford Center is based. It was a wrenching encounter for both of them, but the upside was that the tragedy helped cement the older son's recovery.

Shortly after the 2008 presidential election, while Tom was still in a fog of grief trying to cope with the loss of his younger son, he received a phone call from President-elect Barack Obama, followed by a second call from Vice President-elect Joe Biden, asking him to join the White House team as deputy director of the Office of National Drug Control Policy.

"There couldn't have been anything further from my mind than going into government service," Tom remembered as we spoke. "Anyone who knows me knows I am not cut out for government service. But the more I thought about it, the more it seemed like a sign from God. Here was a chance for me to make amends, to help keep someone else from losing a child to addiction and joining this awful club I had joined."

Tom spent nearly two years in Washington and worked ungodly hours on the addiction and recovery piece of health care reform, the beginnings of a parity act, and a new drug policy, the first to move the needle to bring supply reduction and demand reduction closer together. But what made the most difference wasn't Tom's long, distinguished career in the drug abuse field. It was the tragedy of his loss. In Congressional hearings, the fact that his brother, father, and son had all died from the disease of addiction carried far more emotional weight, and garnered more attention, than any of his academic credentials.

I am glad that pain got me out of my seat and put me in a new position to help make a difference. Doing that public service in my son's memory, I never got over it and a piece of me never wants to get over it. I never want that pain to completely go away, though it does energize you. But I can tell you that it's not worth it. You don't have to experience the kind of devastating loss I did to find a benefit. A job loss, that loss of a friend because you embarrassed him . . . all are opportunities to reevaluate what you want to do with the rest of your life. It doesn't take *extraordinary* pain to do it. Small pains are harbingers of more serious pains that can come. I am not in recovery myself but I have learned so much from the recovery principles, their simplicity and their elegance, the quality of making an impact. They are so much about the exercise of common sense. Whether you are an addict or not, you can apply the lessons of recovery and make a much better quality of life for yourself and those around you.

If you've never failed at anything, so the saying goes, you've probably never attempted anything new. Luckily, most of us have not experienced Tom McLellan's pain. But we all have failures and flops, trials and tribulations. The great achievers, who first had to experience the pain of failure and rejection in order to transform their lives and become great success stories, certainly know that maxim.

Though he was a failing student whose teachers agreed he would "never amount to much," Albert Einstein ignored other people's standards for failure to become one of the greatest scientists in history.

Though he was fired from his job at a newspaper for "lacking imagination and original ideas," Walt Disney bounced back to become one of the most original innovators in the history of movies and entertainment.

Though she lost her job as a news anchor because her superiors thought she "wasn't fit for television," Oprah Winfrey persisted with her dream and vision for her career to become the most powerful woman in the history of the medium.

Being human means we experience pain and failure, some of it imagined, most of it very real. It's an unavoidable fact of life that all of us—particularly people in recovery from addictions—must embrace if personal growth and wellness are to shape our destinies. From pain can come both extraordinary growth and remarkable contributions to community and society.

BOUNCING OFF THE BOTTOM

Hitting rock bottom and how far you bounce up afterward is one measure of a life well spent. Those among us who fell the furthest and bounced back the highest should be beacons of hope and inspiration for anybody ready to give up on goals or life. I want to share a few of these special people with you.

On the January night that Lauri Burns had been kidnapped and left for dead alongside a canyon road, savagely beaten by two gun-wielding rapists, she was a twenty-three-year-old heroin addict and prostitute living on the streets of Southern California. She had grown up in New York in an abusive home and become a foster child, then a ward of the juvenile justice system. She turned to intravenous drugs as a welcome reprieve from her hellish childhood. By the age of nineteen, nursing a serious drug problem and a young child, she had begun selling her body on the streets.

As the two men beat and ravaged her in the darkness, Lauri screamed at them, "Kill me! Kill me!" In many ways, given the struggles in her life, death seemed a welcome release from the pain and suffering.

She awoke from unconsciousness to find a passerby kneeling over her, crying, obviously distraught by her bloody appearance. He rushed her to a hospital.

"A stranger saved my life," Lauri recalled, describing that night for me. "I woke up to a guardian angel."

When she was released from the hospital, Lauri had nowhere to go but back to the streets. She had no one to turn to, so she phoned a client of hers from an escort service she had worked for.

"Fred, can you help me?"

"I will come and get you," Fred replied gruffly. "But I'm not giving you one dime, so don't ask."

Fred didn't resemble any ordinary client of prostitution services. He was a Vietnam veteran confined to a wheelchair, physically incapable of having sex. He had called the escort service months earlier out of loneliness, and Lauri showed up. He had only wanted to take her to a movie.

Fred drove her to a drug treatment center and dropped her off. When she got out of treatment, he let her stay at his house for a few weeks and watched over her, making sure she stayed sober. He had become Lauri's second guardian angel.

Lauri's personal transformation accelerated when she volunteered to work with kids sentenced to juvenile jail for crimes and drug use. "Seeing those kids made me feel at home, like ET glowing when he got close to the mothership. It radiated throughout my life. I saw the new direction my life could take."

Lauri parlayed her natural affinity for math into computer-industry jobs and continued working with teenage girls, using her home as a recovery meeting space for single moms struggling with drug addiction. She became a foster mom and began raising money to create a special home for foster kids who turn eighteen and find themselves homeless.

Today, Lauri Burns owns a computer consulting firm and works for a Fortune 100 defense contractor. The nonprofit organization she began, The Teen Project, has more than sixty committed volunteers working with her in the area of Mission Viejo, California, to provide shelter and counseling for at-risk foster home kids, many of whom have drug or alcohol problems. She said:

> The message for me from my life is that you don't need to be the perfect person to help someone. And you don't need to get feedback that you have been effective. A lot of people planted seeds of hope in me but never knew it. Whether you are on the receiving or giving end of service, you have to realize you are planting seeds.
>
> I am clear on the fact that my life was saved for a larger purpose. All of the bad stuff that happened to me prepared me for the glorious life I now have. I needed those horrible experiences to draw upon, and I use those direct events to reach the kids I work with. The foster kids, the homeless kids, the drug addict kids, they have innate trust for me because they understand where I've been, and they know that I know where they've been. When you find survivors of the same shipwreck, you bond with them. All of that stuff happened to me so I could find someone in more pain and help them.

MEASURING YOUR LIFE'S TENACITY

It's not unusual for people in recovery to hit rock bottom again and again in areas other than their addiction struggles. But being so well-grounded in recovery skills helps prepare them for those other unpredictable pitfalls, when for some reason shit just happens and happens.

Meet Ken Cross. A decade ago Ken led an exciting, financially successful life as the head of physical production for one of Hollywood's largest movie studios, managing its office space and production lot. He had already been in recovery from alcohol and drugs for two decades at that point.

One day at the height of his career, he was diagnosed with a brain tumor. After surgery to remove the malignancy, he had to leave his job for a long year of recuperation. He battled major depression. But no sooner did he begin to improve than he was diagnosed with testicular cancer, followed in succession by kidney cancer and prostate cancer. It was as if life had conspired to deal him the cruelest hand in the health deck.

"Why me?" Ken kept asking himself. "Why is this happening to me?"

He couldn't believe that after all the hard work he had put into his career, and all the equally hard work he had put into his sobriety, that everything could be taken away in the blink of an eye. He was in constant pain, financially broke and feeling broken, rendered jobless and forced to file for Social Security disability. He felt suicidal. He felt like the darkness was closing in and there was no way out.

"I began to question everything," Ken would tell me years later. "I questioned 12-Step programs and my sobriety. I questioned spirituality. I questioned God. I questioned whether life was worth living."

A friend of Ken's who suffered from advanced Parkinson's disease pulled him aside and offered a piece of advice that became a mantra for him: "You can walk through this with dignity, or you can lose your mind. It's your choice."

That old adage "What doesn't kill you makes you stronger" certainly proved true in Ken's case. He reached out to people in the 12-Step community and they showed up for him. With their support, he intensified his working of the steps and deepened his spiritual foundation with spiritual teachers, meditation, and prayer practices. As he put it, "It comes back to acceptance and surrender. I continued to feel there was something, a divine energy, bigger than me that I could draw upon. It was like I had filled a bank account from a lot of recovery that I could draw upon."

Spiritual beliefs and the 12-Step principles carried him through a decade of hellacious medical challenges until he was finally given a clean bill of health in 2012, with all of the cancers in remission. Within the recovery community he is like an icon, someone who always makes himself of service to others.

So often, self-pity takes people out of recovery. It's not that Ken is completely free of resentment about all those challenges, but his perseverance demonstrates how the core principles of recovery can be applied by anyone, within or outside of addiction recovery, to elevate the human condition.

ACCEPT PAIN AS A NATURAL PART OF LIFE

"The severity of a crisis or challenge is determined not necessarily by the traumatic situation or event, but by your reaction to it," explained psychotherapist Terri Cole. "The word 'crisis' in Chinese is formed with the characters for 'danger' and 'opportunity.' A crisis presents traumatic disruption or threat, but it also presents a unique opportunity for growth."

Helen Keller, one of the most extraordinary people in human history, overcame blindness and deafness to connect with the outside world and become a great humanitarian. She wrote these poignant words: "When one door of happiness closes, another opens; but often we look so long at the closed door that we do not see the one which has been opened for us."

There is a gem of self-learning in every one of our painful experiences, and we only need to give up our victim mentality and our preoccupation with what is wrong to find those gems, those blessings in disguise. "Gratitude softens the harsh sting of a crisis or challenge and helps instill hope in your heart," Cole told me. "If you can accept that all experiences, even the ones you do not want, are part of your life journey, you will look at a crisis or challenge through different eyes."

In our culture we are indoctrinated with the idea that pain and failure should be avoided at all costs. But if we buy into that, if we refuse to participate in any experience that might be painful, we deny ourselves the opportunity to experience the joy that is the flip side of pain.

A personal illustration: I am one of those people who love dogs. The big problem with dogs is that they die. They die in a relatively short span—twelve or fourteen years. Is that any reason not to have a dog as your companion, just because you will inevitably feel the pain of loss? Of course not!

Someone once described to me how the experience of pain is a definite part of life's worth, regardless of how much the emotional pain may hurt. That's the first lesson I draw. The second is that when you're lying on your deathbed, I suspect that the painful things you reflect on will often be the most informative of your life, showing you what ultimately got you to where you needed to go. That's the idea behind pain as the touchstone of spiritual growth.

Not only are you going to get closer to a spiritual experience if you embrace your emotional pain, but also get closer to who you are and what your life should be. This is a lesson recovering addicts have learned over the course of sustained recovery.

In 2001, I was diagnosed with hepatitis C, I separated from my wife, and my career was in the toilet, all at the same time. I had to reevaluate everything and radically alter my life. I had to intentionally make it a transformative period for me. I was certainly intentional about not returning to drugs and alcohol. I was intentional about not killing myself or hurting anybody else. So intention has a big life-preserver role to play when you're floundering in a sea of confusion and doubt.

What is your intention? If you've done all the work beforehand about what you want your life to look like and who you want to be, or you have at least initiated that process, you can get through the painful periods and they will, in fact, be transformational.

Two important healing catalysts help facilitate this growth: First, find self-compassion for yourself and, second, get in the habit of feeling and expressing gratitude for what you already have in life.

SELF-COMPASSION ISN'T JUST ABOUT SELF-ESTEEM

Be compassionate to yourself: It's not narcissistic and self-indulgent, and it's certainly not about you lowering your standards or escaping responsibility. Feeling compassion for oneself "entails being kind toward oneself in instances of pain or failure; perceiving one's experiences as part of the larger human experience; and holding painful thoughts and feelings in balanced awareness," concluded a 2007 study that examined levels of psychological functioning in 177 college students.[19]

Dr. Kristin Neff, a coauthor of that study and an associate professor of human development at the University of Texas at Austin,

---

19 Kristin D. Neff et al., "An examination of self-compassion in relation to positive psychological functioning and personality traits," *Journal of Research in Personality* 41 (Aug 2007): 908–16, doi: 10.1016/j.jrp.2006.08.002.

emphasized that giving yourself a break and accepting your imperfections will go a long way toward making you a more optimistic and happier person. It's part of a formula for transforming pain into growth. Sounds simple, doesn't it? So why isn't it happening more often?

"I found in my research that the biggest reason people aren't more self-compassionate is that they are afraid they'll become self-indulgent," Neff explained to the *New York Times*. "They believe self-criticism is what keeps them in line. Most people have gotten it wrong because our culture says being hard on yourself is the way to be."

For those of us in recovery from a toxic compulsion, even a minor shift in attitude about practicing self-compassion can help solidify the healing process. One of the revealing studies affirming this was conducted among problem (and other) eaters at Wake Forest University. The eighty-four college women in the study thought they were taking part in a food-tasting experiment, but it was really about whether feeling self-compassion affected their eating habits.

Half of the students were given a short lesson in self-compassion before being served doughnuts to eat, while the other half received no such instruction. Those study subjects who were regular dieters or who felt guilt about having fattening foods actually ate fewer doughnuts after hearing the researchers say, "I hope you won't be hard on yourself. Everyone in the study eats this stuff, so I don't think there's any reason to feel real bad about it." Those who didn't receive the self-compassion message ate more of the doughnuts and other fattening foods.[20]

---

20 Claire E. Adams and Mark R. Leary, "Promoting self-compassionate attitudes toward eating among restrictive and guilty eaters," *Journal of Social and Clinical Psychology* 26, no. 10 (2007): 1120–44, doi: 10.1521/jscp.2007.26.10.1120.

Self-compassion must be a central element of every recovery-from-addiction plan. It's beneficial for everyone to practice it, whether in recovery or not, because it helps relieve stress, depression, anxiety, and angst about control (or lack thereof) over the challenges of life.

ATTITUDES OF GRATITUDE EMPOWER YOU

We have several expressions —"look for blessings in disguise" and "every cloud has a silver lining"—that are meant to help us cultivate an attitude of gratitude at all times, especially in the face of adversity.

Phillip Valentine, executive director of the Connecticut Community for Addiction Recovery, had this to say about gratitude: "If you're feeling sorry for yourself, go out and help someone. That's a lesson from Twelve Steps. If I get irritated during my day, one technique I am teaching myself is to consciously decide to see the joy and humor in this situation. Will I look at the bright side or dark side? Gratitude lifts. If you're down or discouraged, write a gratitude list. You might only have two things to write down early in recovery, but if you stick with the program your list gets longer. If you have a short gratitude list, that's a sign you need to do some internal work."

Keep in mind that you will always be your own most powerful ally so long as you can keep the negativity from overwhelming you. "Gratitude shifts your perspective from what's missing in your life to what is present," observed psychotherapist Donald Altman in *The Joy Compass: Eight Ways to Find Lasting Happiness, Gratitude, and Optimism in the Present Moment.* "It must have been gratitude that a wise person was referring to when advising, 'Pray for what you already have in your life; that way your prayers will be instantly answered.'

"One of the most crucial and fundamental forms of gratitude—although it often goes unnoticed—is appreciating your own strengths and good qualities." Altman recommends you keep a gratitude journal in which every day, or every few days, you write down everything you are grateful for, including your own strengths and good qualities, along with acknowledgments of people who have shown you kindness or helped you in some way.

By expressing these feelings, you turn gratitude into an effective coping skill that pays dividends for your mental and physical health. Robert A. Emmons, a professor of psychology at the University of California at Davis, has studied how feelings of gratefulness affect us both emotionally and physically. One observable effect is that gratefulness builds social relationships, and people with more social support experience more health and contentment than those without it.[21]

AN EXERCISE TO CULTIVATE GRATITUDE

We can cultivate feelings of gratitude and experience them more frequently by using affirmations.

Whether you realize it or not, you already use affirmations every day. These are statements you repeat to yourself and others that reflect your views. These statements can be either positive or negative; we reflexively use both, but expressing too many negative statements can make us seem depressed and cynical, and a preponderance of positive ones can make us appear as wide-eyed Pollyannas.

The trick is to learn how you can consciously turn negative affirmations into positive ones—and do so until it is second nature.

---

21 RA Emmons and ME McCullough, "Counting blessings versus burdens: an experimental investigation of gratitude and subjective well-being in daily life," *Journal of Personality and Social Psychology* 84, no. 2 (Feb. 2003): 377–89.

Most of us already know all too well how to be self-critical. Positive affirmations train your brain to open up mental channels and welcome more of life's goodness into your reality.

Motivational author Louise L. Hay describes in many of her books how the power of positive affirmations may be used as a self-help tool, and she recommends turning the negatives into positives this way: "If you are saying to yourself something like, I don't want to be unhappy anymore, start saying instead, I am happy."

Transform pain into growth, or adversity into a path to success, by catching yourself every time you think or say, "I am a failure" or "I am a victim," and choose to say instead, "I am blessed beyond measure" or "I am becoming the person I want to be."

This all might seem to be yet another version of that old "fake it until you make it" advice, but repetition of positive affirmations does help condition you over time to generally adopt a more positive attitude.

Feelings of gratitude can be developed by using the same technique. For instance, practice saying, "thank you, life" each and every time you see something beautiful or in some way experience something positive.

Say, "thank you, life" when you see a mother holding a child.

Say, "thank you, life" when you experience a gorgeous sunrise or sunset.

Say, "thank you, life" when you perform or receive an act of kindness.

Make this a habit. Turn this practice into a natural part of who you are.

(For more about Lesson #7, including the results of several research studies, visit our website, www.Recover2Live.com.)

LESSON #7: PARTING SHOT

Pain is on a helluva continuum. Health care folks use that 1 to 10 scale, where 1 is a minor, almost imperceptible discomfort and 10 is screaming and tears. Pain is universal, part of the price of being alive. It can be physical, emotional, spiritual—and all of the above. And no matter where your own pain is on that continuum, there is always someone whose pain is worse.

Some pain you can alleviate; some never goes away. So you soldier on through life, a step at a time, accepting your pain as best you can and helping others deal with theirs. You focus on your blessings and triumphs and you help others do the same.

We're all in this together, and nobody gets out alive.

PRACTICE SERVICE TO OTHERS

> Service to others is the rent you pay for your room here
> on earth.
>
> —MUHAMMAD ALI

At the core of community and service in 12-Step programs is the sobriety sponsor, a role that enriches the lives of both sponsors and the persons sponsored. Imagine if everyone could play or benefit from that role, tailored for all types of needs and pursuits, and the contributions to humanity that would result.

MEET LOUIS GOSSETT JR., Academy-Award winning actor. One hot summer's day in North Hollywood, Lou was speaking to a group of people about the importance of sobriety, what it means to have goals in life, and the satisfaction that comes from achieving them, a subject Lou had come to know quite well since beginning his acting career as a seventeen-year-old on Broadway in the early 1950s.

Lou was outside in the heat as he spoke, and the sun was beating down relentlessly on his bald head. He began to feel faint, and the words weren't flowing as easily as they normally did for this marvelously articulate man. Once he got back inside his car, he took huge gulps of Gatorade but still felt like he was going to pass out.

He began driving home on the 101 Freeway through Los Angeles and had to fight off the overwhelming fatigue every mile of the way. Finally, he slumped over and lapsed into unconsciousness. His car swerved off the highway and crashed. He had suffered sun stroke.

While at the hospital, Lou felt himself leaving his body. His vital functions were shutting down and he could no longer feel his fingers or toes. He was plunging down that tunnel described by so many others who have had a near-death experience. He was destined for that realm beyond waking life.

"Go back, it's not your turn," Lou heard an inner voice say. "You have a new life's work ahead of you."

Doctors revived him and he began the process of recovery, much as he had a year earlier when he was diagnosed with prostate cancer. This time was different. He had undergone a transformation in his thinking, a profound recognition that his life's focus must change. I call it a moment of clarity. Lou interpreted the health challenges as "a sign that God wants me on a path of selfless service."

Lou described his transformation to me this way:

Had I continued to be self-seeking I would be dead today. A daily attitude of gratitude now, that's the big difference between when I was visualizing my life climbing the Hollywood ladder, and re-visualizing my life today in service to others. I had to reestablish my value system. "What's in it for us" replaced "what's in it for me." I had to have the humility to let God do his work in my life. The answer for me came by engaging with humility in selfless service, and that's larger than any Academy Award or Emmy. That is the key to the Kingdom.

It's not just people in 12-Step programs Lou serves and inspires with his time, money, and attention. His vision is now truly global, and he's on a mission to bring recovery principles to all of humanity. Lou put it this way: "Transformation happens through pain and personal disappointments. I had used substances and women and money and fame to try and find a right way of life and none of it worked. There had been no place in my mind to visualize what it means to be humble and selfless, but there was that moment of clarity when I almost died and I got it. We have to grab on to those moments like our life depends on it. School is never going to be out. It's never going to be over. The old diseased thinking doesn't work. It's not an addict's recovery thing anymore. It's about the recovery of the entire planet, because everyone on this planet is on a 747 airplane plummeting to the ground, and it's not important who is in first class."

My spiritual belief is that we're here to be of service to one another. When you're too self-centered and self-focused, it's usually a symptom of unhappiness. If you talk to anybody who centers their life on giving to others, ultimately it's the greatest feeling and the greatest gift, a gift that keeps giving long after the act of service is performed.

Service is when you're thinking about how you can help somebody else in their life, and you do so unconditionally. The payoff never fails: you feel good about yourself and about life.

YOU CAN BE OF SERVICE TO ANYONE

Remember Lauri Burns from Lesson #7, the woman who overcame drug addiction and a near-fatal beating to become a guardian angel for countless foster kids? She had this to say about the impact of helping others: "Everyone in society is in pain at some level. Everyone is pissed off about something in their lives. Being of service can make that bad stuff turn good, like turning shit into ice cream. Because once you are engaged in the act of serving others, none of that petty stuff in your life seems important anymore. You don't necessarily forget it, but it just doesn't hold you back anymore."

No matter how rich you are, you're probably always insecure about money and always want more. The same is true for power and fame. But all of these earthly pursuits don't give what they promise. Service to others does. In a 12-Step recovery program, the greatest gift of service to someone else is to be their sponsor, which in many ways is a mentoring relationship. Some people can get sober without a sponsor, as retired real estate broker and art gallery owner Jack Hoffman noted during a conversation we had, "but it's like someone trying to build a bridge without any engineering background," he said.

Jack has been in recovery from alcohol and drugs for a quarter-century. "It would make sense to have access to someone who has been there and done that. Otherwise, it's all trial and error and the possibility of major failure. Sponsorship in 12-Step programs works. It's a chance to move in a new direction without doing it alone. I tell people to find up to five sponsors because then you realize that everyone has a worthwhile perspective, and all of those perspective maps taken together are more powerful than any one is on its own."

Most people who come to 12-Step programs are consumed with what they've lost in their lives and feeling obsessed with getting it back. They've got bills to pay. Their relationships are in tatters. Their health is bad. They come to 12-Step programs so they can stop behaving destructively and find what they've lost.

Veterans of 12-Step programs will say to them, "Don't worry about all that stuff, it'll take care of itself. You just worry about going to meetings and helping other people." That's at the core of the program, examining yourself, not drinking or doing whatever toxic things you did on a daily basis, and then focusing on how you can be of service to other people. Then life will take care of itself.

Most people don't believe this. They don't understand how going to meetings and helping other people is going to help, much less solve their own unemployment situation, or anything radical like that. But miraculously it does, usually in ways no one could have foreseen. You have to believe that there's some energy in the universe that is going to take care of you. If you don't believe that, you're in serious trouble if you're in recovery from a toxic compulsion.

It's a perspective issue, and one that requires constant vigilance. I remember I would go to job interviews or scheduled appearances and I'd be scared, and people would reassure me, "You just go and look for ways you can be of service there." With this service orientation and mind-set, I didn't feel any of the anxiety I would have had if it was all about me looking good and succeeding.

PLANTING SEEDS, PAYING IT FORWARD

It seemed like such a spontaneously ordinary gesture, yet this one momentary act of kindness planted a seed of hope that helped change the entire trajectory of a woman's life. Meet Penny Vizcarra and Monica Schneider.

Penny was a volunteer facilitating a group session of women during 2007 at Friendly House, a Los Angeles drug and alcohol treatment center that is the oldest operating residential facility for addicted women in the United States.

When the session was over, Penny's attention was drawn to a new arrival, a sad-looking woman with a bruise on her face. Penny walked over to Monica, placed her hands on either side of Monica's face, and said: "I have a feeling you are going to make it. You are going to be a phenomenal addition to Friendly House."

Monica had fallen extremely fast and far in her life. She had been an executive in the fashion industry, owned several retail stores, and had been consulting for Nike, Disney, and other corporations, before alcoholism began to unravel her. Her health had deteriorated from the addiction; she was covered in bruises from passing out and falling; her businesses had all failed; she crashed her car while drunk, got arrested, and ended up in jail. That was when she finally sought help at Friendly House. She had lost everything, especially her self-esteem.

That one encounter with Penny was like a ray of sunshine piercing the heavy darkness of Monica's struggle to survive. "I thought, *Wow, she believes in me. Someone saw some light in me,*" Monica related to me a few years later. "It was something very quick and simple, but her kindness and compassion planted a seed of hope in me at a time when hope had been completely extinguished."

After four months of treatment and sobriety, Monica got a weekend manager's job at Friendly House, putting her business and managerial skills to good use. She had found her true calling. "Getting sober enabled me to find out who I really am," Monica explained. "I am not the glamorous executive I thought I was. That isn't my core. While here I discovered that my core self is about practicing service to others."

Today, Monica is the assistant executive director at Friendly House. Though she makes less than a quarter of the salary she did while in the fashion business, she is a far happier person: "This job saved my life. I got my self-worth back. I am able to invest in human dignity. I try to plant the same sort of seeds with the ladies here as Penny planted in me. I have found that being of service to others got me out of myself, out of my head, out of the bondage to self, because substance addiction is such a selfish disease and the more you focus on your problems the more you feel worthless."

One final thought from Monica that resonates with the theme of this chapter: "What a better world we would have if more people just took their natural feelings toward children, the elderly, the arts, the environment, whatever your passion is, and volunteered a service to others. Even if it's just an hour a week, read to a child at a hospital, work for a community group, find a worthy cause. You will benefit as much as you give benefit."

GIVING GIVES BACK IN MULTIPLE WAYS

Most people are consumed with themselves and their own lives most of the time. Every once in a while they step outside of themselves and focus on other people. Those are great times for them, but it's usually a relatively small part of their life.

"Giving is good for both the recipient and the donor," wrote Tom Rath and Jim Harter in their book *Wellbeing: The Five Essential Elements*. For example, people who give blood to the Red Cross usually report feeling a heightened mood both before and after donating. In a 2009 study using fMRI brain scans, neuroscientists documented that "the regions of the brain that are activated when we receive money glow even brighter when we give money."

Feeling emotionally closer to another person makes it more likely we will engage in the same altruistic behavior again. "When we do things for others, we see how we can make a difference, and this gives us confidence in our own ability to create change," observed Rath and Harter. "Well-doing inoculates us against stress and negative emotions."

The evidence comes from studies showing that altruistic behaviors enhance overall health and longevity. First of all, we must avoid being too preoccupied with ourselves, a self-absorption that promotes social isolation and negative moods and emotional states. Second, and most important, we must begin reaching out to others with our most valuable resource—our time. In doing so, we increase our chances of developing a sense of well-being, of having a life filled with purpose and meaning.

Dr. Stephen Post, a professor of bioethics at Case Western Reserve University, has been studying the life-enhancing benefits of caring, kindness, and compassion. He has discovered evidence that when we give of ourselves, especially if we start young, everything from life-satisfaction to self-realization to physical health is significantly improved, mortality is delayed, and depression is reduced.

In their book *Why Good Things Happen to Good People,* Dr. Post and journalist Jill Neimark discussed research such as a fifty-year study showing that people who are givers during their high school years have better physical and mental health throughout their lives. Other studies show that older people who are givers live longer than those who aren't. Helping others has been shown to bring health benefits to those with chronic illness, including multiple sclerosis and heart problems. People of all ages who help others on a regular basis also feel happier than most people who don't engage in service to others.

Post characterized the expression of gratitude and generosity as a "one-a-day vitamin for the soul" resulting in longer, healthier lives for those who do good deeds and are of frequent service to others. He called this a "karma of the brain," whereby your body physically rewards you for acts of kindness and forgiveness. His book includes a "Love and Longevity Scale" to score yourself on ten ways of generating brain karma, from volunteering to expressing forgiveness to loyalty.

KINDNESS TRANSLATES INTO WILLPOWER

If you perform good deeds, or just imagine yourself being charitable to someone else, you fortify your willpower and at the same time, believe it or not, actually increase your physical strength.

That was the remarkable finding from three innovative experiments conducted in 2009 by Harvard University psychologists who put a large group of volunteers through a series of intention and visualization tests.

In the first study, ninety-one volunteers were told to hold up a five-pound weight as long as they possibly could. Each was given a one-dollar bill for completing the assignment. Half of the volunteers were then asked if they would donate their dollar to a children's charity, and all of them did. The other volunteers weren't asked to give away their money. All of the volunteers then went through a second round of holding the weights. Remarkably, those who had donated to charity were able to hold the weight seven seconds longer on average than those who didn't donate.

A second experiment took the testing a step further. This time, 151 volunteers held a weight as they wrote a fictional story in which they imagined themselves aiding, harming, or having a neutral impact on another human being. Volunteers who imagined themselves actively helping someone in need held the weight five seconds longer than those who imagined having a neutral impact. Another aspect of the findings from this second experiment may surprise or perhaps even alarm you. Those study subjects who fantasized about harming another person held the weight about eight seconds longer on average than those who imagined a neutral outcome, and three seconds longer than the helping-someone group. Researchers attributed this "evildoer strength" increase to participants first having to ignore their consciences, which normally restrained them from doing evil against someone, and that in turn reinforced self-control and, as a byproduct, conferred added tenacity or strength.[22]

As you can probably guess, I would strongly advise you to strengthen your willpower and self-control by engaging in acts of kindness and charity toward others, rather than by just imagining

---

22 Kurt Gray and Daniel M. Wegner, "Moral typecasting: divergent perceptions of moral agents and moral patients," *Journal of Personality and Social Psychology* 96 (March 2009): 505–20, doi: 10.1037/a0013748.

those acts. Engaging will bestow a positive "brain karma" on you while making the world a little bit better place for us all.

(For more about Lesson #8, including the results of several research studies, visit our website, www.Recover2Live.com.)

LESSON #8: PARTING SHOT

The word is "volunteer." Yes, it may sound do-goody, something a washed-up retiree does to make his long days go by. But don't underestimate it. It could just make your long days better than they've ever been. You won't know until you try. The opportunities to volunteer are nearly endless; surely there's one right for you. Volunteer at the library, your local food bank, the VA hospital. Read books for the blind; help someone illiterate learn how to read; drive seniors where they need to go. Help serve meals at a homeless shelter. Teach a class at the youth detention facility.

Too busy? Well, do your volunteer work just once a week or maybe as little as once a month. Those organizations will be happy to take whatever you can give. You'll be giving a gift to yourself as well. Volunteering can turn your inward focus outward. As that old saying goes, you'll lose yourself in something greater than yourself.

LESSON #9

ENGAGE WITH COMMUNITY

> We need a new spirit of community, a sense that we are all in
> this together.
>
> —BILL CLINTON

For those in recovery, being engaged with community
offers a support system of advice and inspiration to help
break the isolation of addiction. Imagine if we all knew
how to transform our communities into dynamic incuba-
tors for life skills that benefit the greater good.

MEET SUSAN FORD. She participated in an intervention that changed the recovery world.

While on a photography assignment, Susan, the twenty-two-year-old daughter of President Gerald Ford and First Lady Betty Ford, accompanied a physician to a camp for kids in recovery from addictions. During the drive back from the camp, she decided to address an issue that had been troubling her.

"I have a friend with a mother who has a substance abuse problem," said Susan. "What would you recommend she do?"

The physician proceeded to give his advice about how to organize an intervention. By the time they got back to Palm Springs, the physician, himself in recovery, couldn't hold back his suspicions any longer. "Susan, you're really talking about your mother, aren't you?"

Susan picks up the story from here: "My father, brothers, and I knew that my mother had a problem. She had fallen a few times, and we could see personality changes in her that disturbed us. She was constantly taking prescription drugs, and starting at five each afternoon, she would begin drinking alcohol. For years we had covered up for her and made excuses for her. As a family we had become very skilled enablers. But we knew we had to do something because we felt like her life was at stake."

On the night before the intervention, Susan, her father, and her brothers all met with the physician and rehearsed what they would say. Interventions are often tricky and the outcomes can go either way, so everyone had to be in harmony with the overall message to heighten the emotional impact.

The next morning, April 1, 1978, they all gathered at the Ford home in Rancho Mirage, near Palm Springs. It was 9 a.m. and Betty was still in her robe. She hadn't yet consumed her morning cocktail of prescription pills. With a startled look on her face, Betty blurted out, "Oh, are you all here for April Fool's Day?"

They sat down in the living room and Susan's father introduced his wife to the two physicians and a nurse who accompanied them. Before each family member had finished expressing their concerns and love for Betty, she broke down and began sobbing. She hadn't realized the pain and hurt her husband and children felt. She had no idea her substance abuse had affected her family so dramatically.

Betty Ford entered a treatment facility, and during her stay Susan and other family members uncovered the true extent of her dependency:

> When we discovered how much medication she was taking, my anger got directed at her doctors because of their over-pre-scribing. We didn't realize how bad off she was until we saw the medicine cabinet and cross-checked the prescription records. She could have died and probably would have if we hadn't done the intervention.
>
> My mother found a new spirituality and a new way of living through recovery. She became religious about doing daily medi-tations. That's how she started each day. It totally centered her. Getting my mother sober was the greatest gift to our family. Everybody got honest, and it gave us the courage to truly love each other unconditionally. It changed the whole family for the better.

As countless people now know, tire company heir and philanthropist Leonard Firestone approached Betty Ford in 1982 about opening a treatment clinic bearing her name in the Palm Springs area. "She only had about four years in recovery when she helped start the Betty Ford Center," explained Susan. "She asked our family if it would bother us that an addictions clinic was named after her. We said no, we were so proud and grateful, why should we be embarrassed."

Just as she had previously promoted women's awareness about breast cancer following her own mastectomy, Betty Ford became a tireless champion for treatment and recovery issues. With her characteristic commitment and enthusiasm, she engaged broader society to reenergize a growing recovery community and in the process became a role model and inspiration for millions of people worldwide.

Susan Ford (Bales) became chairwoman of the Betty Ford Center's board of directors in 2005, continuing the Ford family tradition of service to community. She knows the benefits of community engagement firsthand: "The people I see who do community service are far better off than those who just go in and out of 12-Step program meetings. When I do service I come back and realize how selfish I had been before. Service makes me feel better about me, and about life, and makes me realize what is real and what isn't. My mother lived five minutes away from the Betty Ford Center, and while she was alive she would come over and talk to patients. She stayed involved her entire life at both the individual and community levels."

ACTS OF SERVICE, LARGE AND SMALL

Sometimes even seemingly minor acts of service to a community become deeply personal opportunities for self-transformation. Art gallery owner and retired real estate developer Jack Hoffman saw that phenomenon occur one day in Venice, California, after he purchased sixty used chairs for a 12-Step program meeting hall and sought a volunteer to help him clean and touch up the chairs before setting them out for use.

The volunteer was a guy in his forties, newly sober from cocaine and alcohol abuse, whose mind was still reeling and racing from the effects of addiction withdrawal. Let's call him Craig. As Jack and Craig began cleaning the chairs, Jack commented, "Think of our work this way. From today forward, anyone sitting in any of these chairs was touched by you."

Excusing himself to attend to other business, Jack left Craig alone to clean the remaining chairs. An hour later, Jack returned to find Craig still busily at work, but beaming as if infused with a radiant light.

"I feel incredible," Craig blurted out. "And I don't know what happened!"

Jack laughed and replied, "It's good you don't understand it. There is another world out there other than the one you make up in your mind. You are a part of that other world too."

By losing himself not only in the simple work of the moment but also in the idea that what he was doing mattered to a community of his peers, Craig turned a corner in his commitment to sobriety. "Losing himself opened him up," Jack later explained to me. "It completely changed his perspective on what it means to be active and engaged. He got a lesson in how the cost of paying attention to obsessive thoughts is that you lose the freedom of letting things you may not understand just happen naturally."

There is a saying in recovery that if we do this for fun and we do it for free, it's unconditional. We do it to stay sober and the only way you can stay sober is by giving away what you were given. Pay it forward.

What you soon find out in recovery is that being of service to others in the community becomes an elixir of life. Mostly we're preoccupied with ourselves and this is sort of the paradox: Taking action for others releases you from yourself.

Just as with the opposing forces of light and dark and good and evil, there is also a polarity between isolation and community. "Isolation is about addiction, community is about recovery," Phillip Valentine told me. In recovery since 1987 from alcoholism and cocaine addiction, he is now executive director of the Connecticut Community for Addiction Recovery, which provides support services for people in recovery, including help with getting a job, finding a place to live, forming relationships, and developing life skills.

"When I was on cocaine, I was isolated in the dark with a small light doing crossword puzzles," said Valentine. "When I made the choice to get into recovery, it became about me engaging more with other people, the 12-Step community, who understood my isolation and also understood my self-loathing. That community carried me until I could care for myself, and then I could care for others."

How many people languish in deepening isolation? I fear there are many more than we can ever know, at least until they suddenly decide to seek attention. What can that isolation generate? Undiagnosed addictions, alienation, resentment, depression, and despair—these are but a few of the many repercussions. Then there are the fantasies of gun play, cycles of warped antisocial thinking, deranged explosions of violence at schools, theaters, malls, and places of worship . . . think Columbine . . . Aurora . . . Virginia Tech . . . Newtown . . . Boston.

"It's easier for people to isolate now," continued Valentine. "You can connect impersonally through the Internet and technology, but how well do you really communicate that way? What drove me to isolation was fear, fear of being abandoned, fear of being rejected. Drugs and alcohol took away the fear—until they stopped working for me and I knew I had to seek help. The recovery community taught me how to be a part of a community and how to relate to people.

"When you walk into recovery meetings, the conversations are meaningful. They get to the heart of things right away, unlike what usually happens in the outside world. I love that about recovery, the willingness to be vulnerable and to talk intimately. The relationships in recovery are soul to soul connections. Normal people, by contrast, usually display a lot of fear about intimacy with strangers and are very guarded. A key to health and wellness is acknowledging things are *not* okay. HOW is our acronym: honest, open-minded, and willing. These traits characterize people in the recovery community. We are more accepting of people, slower to judge people, and have an easier time telling you the truth without blame or judgment."

Furthermore, said Valentine, "People in long-term recovery, twenty-plus years or so, have two things in common: They believe in a Higher Power and they are quietly of service to others. To me, service to others is an act of gratitude and being sure of your purpose. You must do it out of humility because otherwise it no longer seems like an act of service. One of the indicators in solid recovery is an increase in integrity and high moral standards, and people by nature are of service to others. It becomes part of your character, part of who you are. You reflexively help someone struggling with groceries, with a flat tire, or whatever you see in normal life. You hold doors open. You brighten people's days by spreading your own joy.

"During recovery, I was diagnosed with stage four cancer of the tongue. I went through thirty-nine radiation treatments, lost my hair, and I could barely walk. What I learned through that was how difficult it was for me when people wanted to minister to me. Someone finally said to me, 'You have been of help to other people, but don't deprive me of the opportunity to be of service to you.' When I first walked into AA, that community cared for me until I could learn to love myself. You must let people genuinely love you when you need to be loved. You have to be of service and also let yourself be served. That is a metaphor for a broader way of living."

In his book *Stake Your Claim to Happiness,* which is "an in-depth analysis of how the Twelve Steps will help anyone find serenity," Francis Fennell noted that if we "join together with small groups of others with problems and goals similar to ours [and use] the 12-Step model for group exploration of the process for a spiritual awakening, we can get the benefit of a variety of perspectives and personal opinions on our journey to happiness. You can encourage the development of such groups within your church or fraternal organization or service club. Therapists can also be encouraged to form such groups. A new way of life . . . can be available to all."

COMMUNITY SERVICE AND THE MYTHIC JOURNEY

Engaging with community means you have a group of kindred spirits around you with similar beliefs as you; people whose values are in alignment with yours.

There are millions of people throughout the world who are oriented to a 12-Step lifestyle. You get supported by these communities when you fail, or when you're not doing it the right way, or you're not doing enough, or you're miserable, or whatever. These are the people around you who understand what you're trying to do and the challenges you face in trying doing it.

A necessary prerequisite to engaging with community is practicing service to others. Countless people have learned this is a vital component of a happy, healthy, successful life. Look at all of the service organizations originating in the United States, whether it's the Rotary, Lions, Shriners, and so on. This country has more service organizations than any other in the world, and the foundation for them all is volunteerism. That tells me there is a huge potential for harnessing this service instinct to create a wider recovery community.

We Americans are oriented toward helping other people, whether it's in volunteerism or in foreign aid programs to less-developed countries. President John F. Kennedy said, "Ask not what your country can do for you—ask what you can do for your country." That was probably the most significant phrase he ever uttered in his public life, the words he's most remembered for.

We could even alter that quote slightly and say, "Ask not what your community can do for you—ask what you can do for your community."

It used to be that going into politics was more about being of public service than it was about personal ambition. I look around today and see many more people who seem to be in government and public life for what they can get out of it instead of what they can bring to it.

My hope is that this book will prompt you to think about your motives. You can be of service to somebody and still be self-interested. Even if you have difficulty stepping outside of your self-interest, if you put yourself in a service situation enough times, it will change your heart.

Mythic stories of heroic journeys go back thousands of years, the ancient Greeks providing many of them, and depict a series of stages the hero must pass through: the adventure, trials and tribulations, escape from danger, an acquisition of new knowledge, and finally, returning home. William L. White, a writer on addiction recovery and policy, has likened recovery to a heroic journey experienced by hundreds of thousands of people who have told their recovery stories. As with the ancient journeys, our modern heroes usually fail the final step of their journeys—giving back their knowledge to the communities they came from.

"Returning to the community calls not just for a physical re-entry into and social acceptance back into the community," wrote White in 2004, "but also acts of reconciliation (healing wounds inflicted upon the community, forgiving the community for its own transgressions) and giving something of value back to the community. For the heroic journey to be completed, those debts and obligations must be paid. Left unpaid, the hero's final act of fulfillment remains unconsummated. Left unpaid, the community loses experience and knowledge that could enhance its own health and resiliency."

White identified five ideas about recovery he felt needed to be "inculcated within communities across America":

1. Addiction recovery is a reality.
2. There are many paths to recovery.
3. Recovery flourishes in supportive communities.
4. Recovery is a voluntary process.
5. Recovering and recovered people are part of the solution; recovery gives back what addiction has taken.

FAKE IT UNTIL YOU MAKE IT

Even if you don't believe in personally performing service for others, act as if you believe and you will begin to change. That's exactly what people with addictions find when they come into a recovery program. They are the most self-centered people in the world. They live on self-interest, that's the core of their disease.

Over time, with exposure to 12-Step programs and their service orientation, self-obsession undergoes a change. People who don't have this toxic compulsion orientation may find that being of service comes much more easily to them.

When actors are playing a particular part in a movie, for instance, they talk about how best to embody that role in order to be believable. It depends on how they were trained, but the Method way is basically to bring yourself back through sensory work to a time that was similar to whatever it is you're trying to create. Let's say you have to play the role of somebody who was traumatized by war, but you've never been in a combat situation. Instead you recall when, back in your childhood, you were traumatized by your parents fighting. Remembering and re-creating that trauma will infuse the role you are playing with the emotional impact needed to make your performance believable.

This doesn't take that much work. What you're simply saying is, "Look, I really want to change my life. I don't know if this book or these people who are talking about this stuff know what they're talking about, but I'm willing to act as if they do."

Just be willing to try the suggestions in this book, whether you believe it's going to work or not. The results may surprise you.

The difference between having a good life and a great one is the level of community well-being. This doesn't happen just because you live in the right sort of community or geographical place. Well-being in a community requires "involvement in community groups or organizations . . . thriving community well-being is about what we do to give back to our community," observed Tom Rath and Jim Harter in *Wellbeing: The Five Essential Elements*.

Participating in community cleanup efforts, joining neighborhood watch, organizing social and charitable events—these are just a few of the possibilities. "When we asked people with thriving well-being about the greatest contribution they had made in their life, with few exceptions, they mentioned the impact they have had on another person, group, or community," noted Rath and Harter.

The authors' three recommendations for how to intensify community well-being are the following:

1. Take your personal mission in life and extend it to contributing to the community.
2. Let other people know what your strengths, passions, and interests are so they can help you identify where you can connect with appropriate causes or groups.
3. Join or organize a community event or group, even if it's a small effort. You have to start somewhere.

PARTICIPATORY MUSIC INSPIRES COMMUNITY SPIRIT

We know from research cited in Lesson #6 that actively playing or dancing to music releases endorphins in the human brain, whereas listening passively to music does not, at least not to the same extent. Other research has taken this finding and expanded it to see whether participatory music can create a spirit of community.

Two studies by a duo of researchers from the Max Planck Institute in Germany examined the effects of synchronized singing and drumming on levels of cooperation and helpfulness among groups of four-year-olds in day care centers.

The first study, in 2009, separated thirty-six children into one of three activities: drumming along with a human partner, playing along with a drumming machine, or listening to a drum sound through speakers. Those children drumming with partners did so with higher accuracy and more coordination than children in the other groups. Social partnerships enhance proficiency.[23]

For the second experiment, the researchers gathered ninety-six preschoolers and paired them up. Half of the teams sang a song while synchronizing their walking steps to music. The other half walked or crawled around without musical accompaniment. Then the children were observed as they played games requiring either cooperative action or helpful actions.

Those children who had played and acted out music as a group were much more likely to engage in cooperative solutions to tasks and to help one another complete other tasks. The synchronized music and movements had stimulated empathic concern, sharing, and connectedness among members of that group.[24]

We see this innate human tendency play out when music is used for group solidarity at dance concerts, sporting events, military parades, funeral processions, and other occasions where harmonizing is utilized, usually unconsciously, to help create group cohesion.

Unfortunately, this power can be harnessed in pursuit of both positive and negative goals. Throughout history we've seen the abuse of techniques developed to generate group solidarity, whether in the form of religious cult groups or the Nuremberg rallies in the 1930s led by Adolf Hitler, when martial music, chanting, and marching in unison became a Nazi exercise in mass propaganda and brainwashing.

23 Sebastian Kirschner and Michael Tomasello, "Joint drumming: social context facilitates synchronization in preschool children," *Journal of Experimental Child Psychology* 102 (March 2009): 299–314, doi: 10.1016/j.jecp.2008.07.005.
24 Sebastian Kirschner and Michael Tomasello, "Joint music making promotes prosocial behavior in 4-year-old children," *Evolution and Human Behavior* 31 (Sep 2010): 354–64, doi: 10.1016/j.evolhumbehav.2010.04.004.

GROUP CONSCIOUSNESS TRANSFORMS LIVES

Engaging with community offers you the potential to transform your life, probably beyond what you ever imagined possible. For example, a professor of psychology, who lectured on psychiatry at Harvard Medical School, conducted a brilliant series of experiments testing whether the "fake it 'til you make it" adage can work in group situations to improve mental and physical health.

Dr. Ellen J. Langer and her graduate students recruited several dozen men who ranged in age from seventy-five to eighty years old, and divided them into two groups, control and experimental, to test the effects that an induced state of mind-mimicking youthfulness can have on the elderly.

Langer brought the two groups of men together for a week at a retreat facility. The two groups were separated. The control group was instructed to talk about themselves only in the past tense. They had only recent photos, nothing from when they were young, and they had access only to media that was current.

In contrast, the experimental group of men was told to act as if they were the person they had been two decades earlier. The photos they were given of themselves to display were taken decades earlier, and their conversations with one another were restricted to what had occurred when they were younger. These were present-tense conversations, as if the events of the past were happening now. Reinforcing these perceptions, they had no access to any stimulation—books, newspapers, magazines, movies, television, or family photos—less than two decades old. Everything they were exposed to, everything they talked about or thought about, was drawn from their youth.

Each day of the experiment the two groups were put through a battery of tests measuring their vision, hearing, taste sensation, perceptions, cognition, and physical strength. The contrasts between the two groups proved nothing short of remarkable. Langer reported the results in her 1990 book *Mindfulness*: "In the experimental group, finger joint flexibility improved by over a third compared to the control group; strength and eyesight, along with cognition scores, all improved for the experimental group but not the controls [group]; experimental group members actually gained height, as if they were standing taller with dignity."

Many signs of aging actually were reversed in the experimental group. Commented Professor Langer: "The regular and 'irreversible' cycles of aging that we witness in the later stages of human life may be a product of certain assumptions about how one is supposed to grow old. If we didn't feel compelled to carry out these limiting mind-sets, we might have a greater chance of replacing years of decline with years of growth and purpose."

Imagine how this group dynamic can play out in other realms of life. We already see it every day in 12-Step groups where the infectious community spirit reinforces healthy abstinence, diminishes stigma and shame, and ultimately transforms lives for the better. Why can't this concept, demonstrated in the Langer experiments on mindfulness, be consciously extended to other areas of broader society and community?

The scenarios are endless. How about applying these principles in church and worship settings to inspire more volunteerism and public service? How about using them to generate more compassion and accountability in prison populations? The possibilities for group change are limited only by our collective imagination.

(For more about Lesson #9, including the results of several research studies, visit our website, www.Recover2Live.com.)

LESSON #9: PARTING SHOT

OK, you say you're not a joiner. Well, maybe you should be. That's the message, of course, of the chapter you just read. You don't have to join the US Army or run away with the circus. But how about getting into something you like? Maybe a book club. Or a walking club. Or a tai chi club. Help local festival organizers. Attend a church. Just do it, as the Nike folks say. Drop that self-centered loner mentality and get out to where the action is. You'll find folks very much like you and folks oh-so-different from you. And that's the whole idea.

MAINTAIN A SPIRITUAL PRACTICE

The foundation of all spiritual practice is love.

—DALAI LAMA

For many if not most people in recovery from addictions, their path to sobriety ultimately becomes a spiritual journey. Whatever your perspective on a Higher Power, imagine how much more harmonious the planet might be if everyone practiced their spirituality without judgment, power-tripping, or evangelizing, much as was taught in the original tenets of the 12-Step tradition.

MEET TOMMY ROSEN, former gambler. In those days, as he sat at Las Vegas casino blackjack tables for up to ten hours at a time, smoking cigarettes and sipping strong black tea laced with refined sugar, Tommy comforted himself with the thought that because he had kicked his major habits of abusing drugs and alcohol a decade earlier, he needed and even deserved the rush he got from gambling.

On one of these trips, in 2003, the thirty-five-year-old former film-industry entrepreneur suffered a double whammy: He lost thousands of dollars at blackjack and a back condition worsened until he was all but debilitated. He returned home to the San Francisco area knowing he had to change his lifestyle or possibly end up a destitute invalid.

What Tommy decided to try on for size was the practice of Kundalini yoga, an ancient spiritual system first brought to the United States in 1969 and known as the Yoga of Awareness for its focus on developing self-awareness and elevating the human spirit. We discussed yoga earlier in this book, specifically laughter yoga in Lesson #6. Yoga, breathing, meditation—they all overlap and they all are helpful and relevant to virtually everything we discuss.

Kundalini yoga, as practiced by Tommy Rosen and so many others, not only involves traditional yoga's multiple body postures (asanas), it also utilizes a holistic and orchestrated pattern of exercises that include movement, vocalized chanting (word repetition to break mind chatter), deep and rapid breath work, and silent meditation. The idea is to harness the power of kundalini, said to be that flow of energy and consciousness existing within each of us, to bring about union with universal consciousness, a concept that we can also interpret as a Higher Power or God presence.

Tommy had been doing his daily Kundalini practice for several months when he woke up one day and realized two things: his back condition had completely healed and he couldn't remember the last time he had even thought about gambling. His urges to smoke cigarettes and consume refined sugar had also simply died away. The old vices were defused. They no longer interested him.

"My thinking had changed and that's when you know something profound has taken place," Tommy told me. "When I feel anxious or worried or fearful, I can sit down and do twenty minutes of breath work and I feel better. I have developed the capacity to change the way I feel. It feels as if my blood chemistry changed by doing Kundalini yoga. I became a new kind of person. The practice cleaned out all of the subconscious crap that had been plaguing me."

Tommy's transformation illustrates some of the practical benefits of adopting a *sadhana,* a spiritual practice. Anyone can use it to heal mind, body, and soul. In that sense, participation in 12-Step programs involves several kinds of *sadhana,* a spiritual inquiry about life, such as engaging in prayer to the God of your understanding, meditation, and even the acts of compiling a daily personal inventory and attending 12-Step meetings regularly.

Many people enter recovery not believing in any concept of God. They can't accept the idea of any kind of higher power or spirit. Some of them may be disillusioned and cynical from being beaten down by their disease, while others think of themselves as rational beings that reject "superstition" in all forms.

What many of these folks do find, however, are substitutes for the belief in God, whether it's the 12-Step meetings or the light-bulb in their rooms or the universe or the ocean waves—whatever it may be, they act as if it has a transcendent meaning and that gives them hope. Acting this out, whether you really believe in it or not, helps harness a force that can infuse your life with purpose. For addicts, this contributes to prevention of relapse.

In Lesson #2, you met Jack Grisham, the West Coast punk rock band leader who turned his life around after years of alcohol and drug abuse. During more than two decades of recovery, he faced his share of challenges that could have triggered a relapse.

During the summer of 2009, for example, after the clothing store he owned with his ex-wife got hammered out of business by the recession, Jack found himself homeless, jobless, and bankrupt, sleeping in his Toyota Corolla behind a Starbucks dumpster. He took showers at the beach along the Pacific Coast Highway.

"I was grumbling, there's no doubt about that," Jack laughed, describing his circumstances to me:

> One reason I didn't relapse is that my emotional definition of alcohol and drugs had changed. To most people, getting high means release and being carefree. My definition of using was that I might slit my wrists, shit my pants, or end up in jail and be com-pletely screwed. It was never an option for me to relapse.
>
> Spiritually during that time, I had healed enough that I real-ized where I lived isn't really where I lived. Yes, I lived in my car, was bankrupt and divorced, showering at the beach. But I had straightened out enough where I didn't see any of that as anything other than an uncomfortable living situation. My mind was free despite my circumstances. At some level in the realm of spirit, I knew it didn't matter. I would be fine. I might feel sorry for myself for a little while, but I would just laugh and that went away. I was

only down physically. I was never down spiritually. I had ingested so much spiritual medicine during recovery that the low points just didn't matter anymore.

Jack bounced back, as his spiritual conditioning had prepared him to do, going through training to become a clinical hypnotherapist and having a biographical novel he had written, *An American Demon,* optioned for a movie.

There are plenty of people in 12-Step programs who are agnostic or atheist. You don't need a spiritual connection for all twelve to work, but it helps. As Jack's story illustrates, embracing the spiritual dimension of life is a foundation that definitely helps navigate the unpredictable challenges of being human.

PRACTICAL BENEFITS OF A SPIRITUAL PATH

For more than fifteen years Herb Kaighan has conducted 12-Step workshops all over the United States and the world to teach and demonstrate the benefits of walking a spiritual path, regardless of a person's religious beliefs or whether or not they are in recovery from an addiction. He had studied to be a Catholic priest but, as he told me, "I didn't find spirituality. I found friendship and knowledge and dogma, but it didn't change me to be more spiritual. It was only when my alcoholism humbled me sufficiently that I was willing to deal with the alcohol and my spiritual thirst at the same time. My spiritual awakening was a slow process that only began after admitting that I was an alcoholic."

Kaighan tells his workshop participants that embracing a spiritual path is "very practical," with results that can be felt and observed, especially in relationships with others. "It's nothing magical. It's a change in the way we think and feel and behave.

It's done to us and not by us. It's a transformation process. Once you realize at the deepest level that we are one-hundred percent responsible for our feelings and behavior, your anger is diminished or eliminated, your fear is reduced, and a rigorous honesty comes about. We don't lose our ego or our pride or lust. All those human characteristics are still there. But the context changes and we are better able to manage our consciousness."

Though he began the spiritual workshops for people in 12-Step recovery from drug and alcohol dependency, he has seen the participant base expand to include people with gambling, sex, and eating disorder problems, along with folks just curious about how to be spiritual without necessarily being religious. "People without addictions have many of the same sorts of life challenges and relationship issues that people in recovery have," Kaighan pointed out. "Brokenness is the human condition. Fear, reactivity, being in a stuck place, all of that is part of the human condition and can be made easier by a transformation of the human spirit. I know from my own experience, and as most people who complete my workshops also find out, the more we have an authentic relationship with the spiritual and the more we are in service with compassion for other people, the more content we become. That's really important in a culture like the United States where the bars for assessing happiness are so high and unrealistic."

To elaborate further, Kaighan made this observation in his 2010 book, *Twelve Steps to Spiritual Awakening: Enlightenment for Everyone*:

Although pain is inevitable—an intrinsic part of the human condition—suffering is optional. Suffering comes not from life's constant changing, but from our resistance to the change. We live in a culture whose mantra is to "feel good" in all areas of our personal life at all times. We are trained to be "feel good" junkies.

Our spiritual aspirations are soaked in this cultural influence. The reality is that spirituality is not a call to personal comfort, personal peace, or personal happiness. Spirituality is a call to personal *freedom*. Spirituality is an invitation to consciousness, as you answer: *Who am I? Why am I? How do I achieve my purpose?* It is a journey to know your story, your real story—not the myth you've created.

People who engage with community tend to find a spiritual connection to life more readily than people who are isolated and alone. Paul on the road to Damascus finding spontaneous spiritual enlightenment is a rare phenomenon, so most of us need to find long-term spiritual meaning in our connections with other human beings.

I'm talking from the vantage point of somebody who's had a lot of trouble with relationships. I've done it very imperfectly. Being spiritual doesn't necessarily mean everything is fine and good and you live happily ever after. It can be messy. It can be conflicted. What counts most is the willingness to stay in the process, however uncomfortable it might be, to learn what you need to learn.

WHAT DOES "SPIRITUAL" MEAN TO YOU?

Most scientists are thought of as atheists who worship at the altar of rationality and the scientific method. But there are notable exceptions. Arguably the most brilliant scientific mind in human history belonged to Albert Einstein, who had this to say about a Higher Power: "To know that what is impenetrable to us really exists, manifesting itself as the highest wisdom and the most radiant beauty, which our dull facilities can comprehend only in the most primitive forms—this knowledge, this feeling, is at the center of true religiousness. In this sense, and in this sense only, I belong to the ranks of the devoutly religious men."

At the core of Alcoholics Anonymous and other 12-Step programs is the idea of putting faith in a God "as you understand Him." Having a religious outlook or a belief in a Supreme Being isn't a requirement for membership in AA; the only requirement is your desire to stop drinking alcohol.

You can even treat AA or any 12-Step program as your own personal Higher Power, a power greater than yourself, if you so choose. Though AA isn't a religion, it is fundamentally a spiritual organization with reliance on spiritual principles, in whatever way you choose to define the word "spiritual."

Addictions treatment specialist Francis Fennell, who spent a half-century in AA maintaining continuous uninterrupted abstinence, never developed "a strong belief in a personal God," as he wrote in *Stake Your Claim to Happiness*. "I knew of many others personally who have done the same." Fennell noted that although most AA meetings begin and end with a recital of either the Lord's Prayer or the Serenity Prayer, "For nonbelievers, it is a procedure accepted with grace out of respect for the large majority who do believe. In turn, no believer looks askance at those who choose silence as an alternative. Mutual respect for another's opinion is an integral part of the AA program."

In his 2009 book *Recovery: The Twelve Steps as Spiritual Practice*, Rami Shapiro, rabbi and recovering compulsive overeater, offered this description of spiritual growth: "An ever-deepening capacity to embrace life with justice, compassion, curiosity, awe, wonder, serenity, and humility . . . a specific belief in or idea of God is not essential either to spiritual growth or to working the Twelve Steps . . . spirituality isn't something you are, but something you do . . . spirituality refers to behaviors designed to free you from the delusion that your life can be controlled and the illusion that you are controlling it."

Spirituality can have many forms, and just because you're in conflict or things aren't working out so great in your life doesn't mean spirituality isn't working on you and for you. Look at the people who most visibly embody a spiritual life. Many of them spend a lot of time alone in some form of cloistered environment. They go off into nature so they can stay focused on the spiritual pursuit. But even if you're sitting in a cave alone, you're still going to have some personal, unresolved issues.

As long as you're doing the work and you're engaged and you're learning what you need to learn in order to get the life you need to have, you're an example of faith in practice.

The spiritual practice can come in the form of service to others and engagement with community. Your spiritual practice can look like just about anything. It's an energy you connect to that's not of this world. God is within, and spiritual teachers and gurus are simply people who have a stronger understanding and experience of the spiritual path, people who will help you navigate your own way, as if they're shining a flashlight, giving you guidance in the dark.

Some renew their commitment to a spiritual path with activities that are, ironically, physical. In his 2012 book, *Running Ransom Road: Confronting the Past One Marathon at a Time,* Caleb Daniloff described how he uses running as part of his spiritual growth:

> Accessing a spiritual side of yourself is, in my view, an essential component for successful recovery—in other words, tapping into something inside, something bigger than yourself, slightly mysterious, that is beyond judgment and isn't fully knowable but can be felt.

Running had infused a necessary spiritual weight into my life. Running had cracked me open, letting light into the hard-to-reach corners. It was a confessional, baptism by sweat. You can't be false when your legs are screaming, your heart pounding, mouth gaping. You feel naked and when you feel naked you feel naked in front of something. Perhaps God or some cosmic energy or simply the wonder of nature, but something bigger than yourself, stirring a need to honor.

Whatever gets your spiritual juices flowing, so to speak, is rooted in four insights that AA and its founders borrowed from "the teachings of spiritual thinkers from all ages and traditions," noted Ernest Kurtz and Katherine Ketcham in their book, *The Spirituality of Imperfection: Storytelling and the Search for Meaning.* These guiding insights, or "truths that must be rediscovered, sometimes on a daily basis, by each person interested in spirituality," are as follows:

1. First, spirituality is essential to recovery "but different from what anyone imagines it to be."
2. Second, spirituality isn't about magic but about "the wonder inherent in mystery and miracle."
3. Third, spirituality is "more at home with questions than with answers."
4. Finally, true spirituality must "pervade every aspect of one's existence."

Those of us in the recovery community have seen firsthand how believing in a power greater than ourselves does indeed bring hope to people who have felt hopeless. That belief in a Higher Power has proven to be one of the keys to successful recovery from addiction. Outsiders and newcomers to 12-Step programs often hear the terms "spiritual" and "Higher Power" and immediately think of the traditional concepts of religion and God and the pursuit of holy perfection. But as authors Kurtz and Ketcham pointed out, AA (and other 12-Step programs) isn't "a program of perfection but a way of life that accepts imperfection as imperfection. This isn't a room full of saints, but a fellowship of sinners . . . the spirituality of the weak and the broken, the poor and the humble."

Swiss psychiatrist Dr. Carl Jung intuited a connection between spirituality and recovery from addictions, as revealed by his correspondence with AA cofounder Bill Wilson. "You see," Jung wrote in a 1961 letter to Wilson, "alcohol in Latin is 'spiritus' and you use the same word for the highest religious experience as well as for the most depraving poison." It's no coincidence that alcohol has historically been known as "spirits." Alcohol dependence, in Jung's view, was "the equivalent, on a low level, of the spiritual thirst of our being for wholeness."

Addicts want to believe in a form of magic typified by the quick fix of self-medication, and they are in denial that quick-fix shortcuts are a dead end, which also happens to describe many normies in their pursuit of money and material possessions to fill their spiritual vacuum. True and lasting recovery means giving up the search for magical solutions and surrendering to the mystery and miracles of a spiritual path. This teaches us both the limits and the responsibilities of what we are capable of in this earthly realm.

Again, Kurtz and Ketcham weigh in:

Spirituality is one of those realities that you have only so long as you seek it; as soon as you think you have it, you've lost it. In rediscovering this basic spiritual insight, the earliest members of Alcoholics Anonymous tapped the essence of open-endedness that characterizes a spirituality of imperfection. Spirituality is boundless, unable to be fenced in. We do not capture it; it captures us . . .

just as we cannot capture spirituality, so we cannot "seize" an identity. Identity captures us, overtaking us, especially in moments of pain and anguish—when we are lost and searching, stumbling and falling.

Spirituality itself is a gift. No one "earns" spirituality, no one can acquire it or possess it, for spirituality is a reality spontaneously, freely given, and gratitude is the only possible response to that gift.

In that sense, expressing gratitude is a necessary cornerstone of spirituality and any spiritual practice, and that holds true whether you are in recovery from an addiction or not. It's just more visceral and urgent for most of us in recovery because, as Sterling T. Shumway and Thomas G. Kimball pointed out in their book, *Six Essentials to Achieve Lasting Recovery,* the initiation of recovery is often a "moment of clarity," which in and of itself is a "spiritual awakening."

Most people in recovery adopt some form of prayer or meditation practice. Gandhi said, "Prayer is not asking, it is a longing of the soul. It is daily admission of one's weakness." When you admit your weakness, the strength that emerges can be absolutely amazing. People in recovery believe in a personal spirituality, which is possible for anybody. This is one of the greatest lessons for humanity from the collective recovery experience.

SCIENCE AFFIRMS HUMANKIND'S SPIRITUAL NATURE

When I was seventeen or so years into my recovery, I began speaking about addiction and recovery to various groups of people. At a Cape Cod conference of addiction, treatment, and recovery experts, including some from the field of neuroscience, I told the story of my spiritual awakening in 12-Step recovery.

I had been going to meetings for about thirty days in New York City and still had the obsession to drink and use drugs. A guy who was getting sober with me, my first sponsor, told me, "Go home and throw your shoes under the bed."

"Why would I want to do that?" I asked.

"So you can get on your knees and ask a power greater than yourself to remove the obsession with drugs and alcohol."

At this point I was willing to do anything anybody suggested. I had no spiritual contact with God at all then. I had rejected the Catholicism I grew up with. So I went to my room in my mother's home, where I was living at the time, embarrassed and humiliated beyond belief. I pulled the curtain closed so no one would see me, and got on my knees and prayed for deliverance from the cravings. I did that every day for thirty or forty days, and the obsession that had shackled me for seventeen years just vanished.

I considered it a miracle, and it convinced me there was something spiritual in this world. So I told that story to the room full of experts at Cape Cod, and when I was finished, one of the neuroscientists came up to me and said, "I like that moment-of-clarity story you told. We believe that thing you call God is actually a switch in your brain that somehow got tripped."

"That's an interesting theory and I hope you find that spot in the brain one day," I replied. "Even if you do find it, I will still continue to believe there is a God because it works for me."

Ever since that day in New York when I got down on my knees, I have looked for evidence of spirituality in my life, and it has always shown up in undeniable ways. This perspective is available to anybody, if you choose to practice it. I haven't seen anyone in recovery fail to find this spiritual perspective if they really want to, but I've seen plenty of people who refuse to believe and, in my estimation, their experience is diminished and the road they trudge becomes more difficult. Having a spiritual connection makes your life more magical, and the challenges you face grow easier.

If you already believe we humans are hardwired by God or by evolution to be spiritual and have spiritual experiences, you can safely skip this section of the book because the information in it won't surprise you. But for those who constantly seek scientific validation for any assertion, please read on.

Neuroscience research over the past decade has documented specific areas of the human brain most directly involved in creating—or projecting and interpreting—spiritual experiences, revealing how we humans are "wired" to feel spiritual and to periodically sense the divine in everyday life.

The "God Spot" was initially hypothesized in the early twenty-first century as a specific area of the human brain that instills and controls religious belief. It was thought to be located in the temporal lobes, large sections of the brain located over each ear. This initial research was done with temporal-lobe epileptics who tended to report intense religious experiences while suffering seizures.

Subsequent studies using fMRI machines on volunteers discovered that there was no one God Spot, but rather multiple areas of the brain interacting simultaneously that produce the feeling states of spiritual experiences.

In the view of evolutionary biologists, we humans may have developed this capacity for spiritual experience as a coping mechanism to strengthen community cohesion and improve our chances for survival. That's simply one point of view. It's just as feasible to say, it seems to me, that we have this capacity for spiritual experience embedded in our brains, making us innately spiritual beings, because a Higher Power decided to heighten our awareness of its presence permeating all universal consciousness.

Whatever the ultimate reason for our spiritual programming, it's clear from the available research that people interpret the brain signals in different ways, according to beliefs and cultural conditioning. It's possible, as atheists demonstrate in these brain imaging experiments, to override those signals, or to simply interpret them as feelings of personal transcendence or awe at the mysteries of the universe, rather than embrace them as belief in God or a Higher Power.

For the purposes of recovery and 12-Step programs, these research findings reinforce what was already intuitively known from observation and practice—our spiritual dimension can be the foundation for self-transformation. It can get us where we need to go.

Meditation Makes You More Productive

WHEN THE *Harvard Business Review* begins dishing out meditation advice to its corporate business and MBA readers, you know the practice has truly gone mainstream.

"Meditation makes you more productive," read an October 2012 *Review* article. "Meditation brings many benefits: It refreshes us, helps us settle into what's happening now, makes us wiser and gentler, helps us cope in a world that overloads us with information and communication, and more."

How does meditation make business people more productive? "By increasing your capacity to resist distracting urges," said the article.

As it strengthens your "willpower muscle," meditation makes you better equipped to manage distractions and resist

cont'd. on next page

cont'd. from previous page

the urge to be reactive in ways that end up being counter-productive. That capability will "improve your relationships, increase your dependability, and raise your performance . . . you can make better, more thoughtful decisions."

Meditation helps you ask questions and discuss problems more rationally, rather than rant and yell at someone for making a mistake; it enables you to listen rather than blurt out something counterproductive in business meetings; it takes emotion out of buying and selling stocks; it helps keep you focused on tasks at hand rather than compulsively checking text messages and e-mails every few minutes.

PALM THE PRESENT MOMENT—A MEDITATION

I could devote an entire book to describing the benefits of meditation practice, and you've seen it praised often in these pages. But suffice it to say, as Kevin Griffin pointed out in his book *One Breath at a Time: Buddhism and The Twelve Steps,* "Meditation gives us a tool for recognizing the truth in the moment, making it possible to avoid a great deal of potential suffering." It's an "intensely practical tool," he wrote, a way to "support and heal my mundane existence: a tool for developing calm, acceptance, self-inquiry, and examination. And while sometimes I have experiences of great joy and bliss in meditation, [it] is more of a sideshow. The real meat—or tofu, if you prefer—is the way that meditation helps me to connect with my own inner wisdom and thus engage more fully with my life."

"Let a thousand flowers bloom" might apply to the practice of meditation because countless forms are available for sampling and experimentation.

Donald Altman, a psychotherapist and author based in Portland, Oregon, prepared the following "portable grounding meditation," advising that you use it whenever you begin feeling anxious, worried, and overwhelmed, or become lost in negative thoughts. In other words, the following practical meditation is for use in everyday life:

Sit in a comfortable chair and take a couple of nice, long, calming breaths.

Now, just raise your hands up to the height of the heart center, with the palms facing one another. Slowly bring the hands closer until you feel even the slightest or subtle sensation of pressure, heat, or warmth. Stop when you feel this, and just notice this for a few moments.

Then, bring the palms closer until just the fingertips come together with the most feathery, lightest touch. Imagine that the molecules from the fingertips of your right hand are dancing with the molecules of the fingertips of your left hand.

Now, gently bring your palms together until they lightly touch. As you do this, notice how the fingers straighten out and how more heat builds up between the palms. After a few seconds of having the palms touch, raise your elbows up to the side and press your palms together harder—using only about fifteen percent of the total pressure you could exert. Observe how far up your arm the tension goes (does it go to the wrists, elbows, shoulders, etc.).

Now, press your hands together even harder. Do you feel even more heat building in the palms of your hands? Which muscles are tense? After about five seconds of this, let your hands, shoulders, and arms release all this tension. Notice how nice it is to let go of tightness in the body.

Very slowly open your palms, like flower blossoms opening to the morning sun. Sense the coolness in your palms as the heat dissipates.

Finally, let the weight of gravity tug on your hands and arms, letting these gently fall like leaves from a tree, until they come to rest on your lap or legs. Rest for a few more moments in appreciation of your body, which is a precious gift that follows your commands and carries your consciousness so you can achieve your life goals.

———————

(For more about Lesson #10, including the results of several research studies, visit our website, www.Recover2Live.com.)

LESSON #10: PARTING SHOT

Check to see what time the sun rises tomorrow. Set your alarm for about fifteen minutes before that. Then when that annoying buzzer goes off, get dressed appropriately—whatever the season—and take a half-hour walk in your neighborhood. It's the dawn's early light. In my opinion, daybreak is the most magical, even mystical, time of the day, any day, every day.

Don't think too much as you walk; don't force some phony epiphany. Just let the changing light and soft quiet roll over you and envelop you. Spirituality is where you find it.

AFTERWORD:

CHANGING ONE PERSON AT A TIME

A small group of awakened people can change the world. Indeed, it is the only thing that ever has.

—MARGARET MEAD

"Enlightenment" is a tricky and often misunderstood word. It's not always easy to define, at least not to everyone's satisfaction, because it may seem New Agey, even presumptuous. It's a word that tends to trigger alarm bells in rationalists, as well as in some people who think of themselves as traditionally religious.

To me, enlightenment means being able to honestly look at your life's "stuff" and occasionally elevate beyond it, with feelings of bliss and calm. Obviously, there are gradations of this experience, and most of us will only get glimpses. But at its core, it's the idea that everything in the moment is perfect and OK. It's about pure consciousness, the clearing of chatter from your mind. The word "enlightenment" captures the essence of all that, yet it is so much more.

Psychology Tomorrow magazine describes enlightenment as "a complex and multi-faceted process by which the mind comes to know—and over time rest more securely in—its own ground. As this happens, our habitual sense of being a separate and bounded self begins to fade." Along the way, a person no longer feels like an autonomous entity looking out at an external world like a goldfish peering through its glass bowl. People who report experiencing this natural process say they feel a liberating sense of freedom, ease, and spontaneity, which makes enlightenment sound a lot like what many people in recovery from toxic compulsions experience and report—the jump-starting of a process of self-transformation that lands you on a path of spiritual development you never expected or even imagined possible. The result can be an elevated consciousness that brings more contentment into your life and greater harmony with the people around you.

Anybody with the illness of addiction is either trying to medicate something because they feel so much, or they're searching for something meaningful to hold on to, which is in keeping with something actor Richard Dreyfuss once told me: "What addicts are really trying to do is touch the hand of God."

While I don't think we addicts are necessarily aberrations, we are extreme. We take what is human and take it up a couple of notches. You'll often hear addicts talk about how they feel more than other people. I don't know whether that's true or not, but I would say that, generally speaking, although everybody feels the same stuff to varying degrees, addicts seem to feel it more and don't deal with it as well, at least not when using their toxin of choice.

People who get into recovery can take this remarkable capacity for feeling and turn that empathy into enormously useful pursuits. A person in recovery can go into service jobs and bring passion and interpersonal gifts, or they can become amazingly creative.

They have a capacity honed by wrestling with their addiction demons to become exceptional human beings. They can turn all of that self-destructive energy toward something productive. This is what I've seen. That has been my experience.

Folks on the recovery road are consciously, on a daily basis, aware of how they're living with respect to the lessons in this book. They must continually monitor themselves because recovery depends on self-scrutiny. Once addicts take responsibility for their thoughts and actions, they must develop an overlay of love, tolerance, and service to others in order to deepen and solidify their recoveries. How often and under what circumstances does this sort of transformation occur within broader society? Not often enough.

WHAT SOCIETY CAN BENEFIT FROM KNOWING

Addicts in recovery understand that you can get rewards from money, people, places, and things, but nothing can replace being of service to your fellow humans. Addicts know that organizations or a community can work without appointed or elected leaders and self-styled gurus. They know that human beings will ultimately disappoint you, and that if you live by spiritual principles that are time-tested, you'll be a more contented person.

Addicts know that no matter how diminished they are or how sick they're labeled, they can become well. Addicts can, in fact, become exceptional. You don't ever have to give up on yourself or anybody else. Those in recovery learn that there are people on the planet who would do anything for them, without wanting anything in return. They come to believe in the power of *we*—the idea that contact with a group of like-minded people can deliver individuals to a higher consciousness. You don't have to do it all by yourself.

How can society be transformed by paying attention to the collective lessons and practices of recovery? I put that question to Geoffrey S. Mason, a recovery role model. This twenty-six-time Emmy Award winner and former executive producer of ABC Sports has served for twenty-two years on the board of the Betty Ford Center and enjoyed success in every area of his life since entering recovery from alcohol abuse.

"There is a huge payoff to your life in doing the 12-Step work," said Geoffrey. "I feel bad that more people don't have the same opportunity that those of us in recovery do to understand ourselves more honestly and to act more honestly. I feel sorry for people who haven't attacked themselves the way we have in the program, to disgorge the artificiality of life and get the poisons out of our systems. I wish other people could have the opportunity to do just a small part of the work on themselves that we do every day in recovery programs. The whole world would be better off."

When we talk about the future of humankind and creating a new planetary consciousness, it seems utterly impossible and overwhelming—until we realize that it's really about changing just one person and one life at a time.

Change will happen incrementally. It's already happening in the way many of us eat and exercise. Are we more conscious of our food choices and the importance of those choices for our health than we were just a few decades ago? Yes, for sure. Making wise choices about what we choose to put into our bodies and the consciousness those choices require—this is all beginning to change the world for the better.

I've had nearly every kind of experience imaginable—seen my ship come in financially and been blessed in so many other ways—yet nothing compares to the feeling of doing this book's lessons and having the transformational epiphanies that result. These lessons can give or restore to you contentment.

I have seen people in 12-Step programs reach out a hand to someone who needs it and alter that person's life. Radical regeneration occurs in these programs. People undergo extraordinary spiritual renewals.

My family legacy includes the certitude that "one man can make a difference and every man should try." All of my uncles truly believed that, and it energized their commitments to public service.

If you want to change the world, first change yourself. This book's ten principles—its ten lessons—are a good place to start.

APPENDIX:

TWELVE STEPS AND TWELVE TRADITIONS

As a refresher for those of you in recovery from toxic compulsions, or as an introduction to those of you non-addicts curious about the foundational principles for all of the various 12-Step programs, here is a short description of the Twelve Steps and the Twelve Traditions as first compiled in 1952 by Bill Wilson, cofounder of Alcoholics Anonymous.

Other 12-Step–based groups have been created for sexual compulsions, drug addiction, overeating, etc. They simply replaced the word "Alcoholics" with the name of their own particular toxic compulsion. So simply insert your area of personal concern into each of the steps and traditions:

THE TWELVE STEPS

STEP ONE: We admitted we were powerless over alcohol—that our lives had become unmanageable.

◆

STEP TWO: Came to believe that a Power greater than ourselves could restore us to sanity.

◆

STEP THREE: Made a decision to turn our will and our lives over to the care of God *as we understood Him.*

◆

STEP FOUR: Made a searching and fearless moral inventory of ourselves.

◆

STEP FIVE: Admitted to God, to ourselves, and to another human being the exact nature of our wrongs.

◆

STEP SIX: Were entirely ready to have God remove all these defects of character.

◆

STEP SEVEN: Humbly asked Him to remove our shortcomings.

◆

STEP EIGHT: Made a list of all persons we had harmed, and became willing to make amends to them all.

◆

STEP NINE: Made direct amends to such people wherever possible, except when to do so would injure them or others.

◆

STEP TEN: Continued to take personal inventory and when we were wrong, promptly admitted it.

◆

STEP ELEVEN: Sought through prayer and meditation to improve our conscious contact with God as we understood Him, praying only for knowledge of His will for us and the power to carry that out.

◆

STEP TWELVE: Having had a spiritual awakening as the result of these steps, we tried to carry this message to alcoholics, and to practice these principles in all our affairs.

• • •

THE TWELVE TRADITIONS

TRADITION ONE: Our common welfare should come first; personal recovery depends upon AA unity.

◆

TRADITION TWO: For our group purpose there is but one ultimate authority—a loving God as He may express Himself in our group conscience. Our leaders are but trusted servants; they do not govern.

◆

TRADITION THREE: The only requirement for AA membership is a desire to stop drinking.

◆

TRADITION FOUR: Each group should be autonomous except in matters affecting other groups or AA as a whole.

◆

TRADITION FIVE: Each group has but one primary purpose—to carry its message to the alcoholic who still suffers.

◆

TRADITION SIX: An AA group ought never endorse, finance, or lend the AA name to any related facility or outside enterprise, lest problems of money, property, and prestige divert us from our primary purpose.

◆

TRADITION SEVEN: Every AA group ought to be fully self-supporting, declining outside contributions.

♦

TRADITION EIGHT: Alcoholics Anonymous should remain forever nonprofessional, but our service centers may employ special workers.

♦

TRADITION NINE: AA, as such, ought never be organized; but we may create service boards or committees directly responsible to those they serve.

♦

TRADITION TEN: Alcoholics Anonymous has no opinion on outside issues; hence the AA name ought never be drawn into public controversy.

♦

TRADITION ELEVEN: Our public relations policy is based on attraction rather than promotion; we need always maintain personal anonymity at the level of press, radio, and films.

♦

TRADITION TWELVE: Anonymity is the spiritual foundation of all traditions, ever reminding us to place principles before personalities.

• • •

ACKNOWLEDGMENTS

My profound thanks to Dr. Drew Pinsky for his elegant Foreword and for his intelligent and empathic advocacy for all those struggling to find their recovery. My thanks to my collaborator, Randall Fitzgerald, for his tenacious creativity and relentless effort, without which this book would not exist. To Glenn Yeffeth and the entire BenBella team for their support and commitment to excellence in publishing. And to our editor, Brian Nicol, who once again brought years of experience and a stellar talent to these pages and made them better. And lastly, I want to express my profound gratitude to all those who shared their recovery with me, for your honesty and the trust you placed in me. Your courage in sharing what you have learned will change the way society views recovery and will inspire those who are struggling to get there.

ABOUT THE AUTHOR

Christopher Kennedy Lawford spent twenty years in the film and television industries as an actor, lawyer, executive, and producer. He is the author of three *New York Times* best-selling books: *Symptoms of Withdrawal: A Memoir of Snapshots and Redemption* (2005), *Moments of Clarity* (2009), and *Recover to Live* (2013). He has also published *Healing Hepatitis C* (2009).

In recovery for more than twenty-six years from drug addiction, Mr. Lawford campaigns tirelessly on behalf of the recovery community in both the public and private sectors. He currently works with the United Nations, the Canadian Center on Substance Abuse, the White House Office on Drug Control Policy, and the World Health Organization. He also consults with Fortune 500 companies and numerous nonprofit groups, speaking around the world on issues related to addiction, mental health, and hepatitis C.

In 2009, California Gov. Arnold Schwarzenegger appointed Mr. Lawford to the California Public Health Advisory Committee. In 2011, Mr. Lawford was named Goodwill Ambassador for the United Nations Office on Drugs and Crime to promote activities supporting drug treatment, care, and recovery. He also serves as National Advocacy Consultant for Caron Treatment Centers.

Mr. Lawford holds a bachelor of arts from Tufts University, a juris doctor from Boston College Law School, and a master's certification in clinical psychology from Harvard Medical School, where he held an academic appointment as a lecturer in psychiatry. Mr. Lawford has three children and lives in Los Angeles.

INDEX